Exploring Manitoulin

Exploring
Manitoulin

THIRD EDITION

Shelley J. Pearen

UNIVERSITY OF TORONTO PRESS
Toronto Buffalo London

© University of Toronto Press Incorporated 1992
Toronto Buffalo London
Printed in Canada
Reprinted 1993

Revised edition published 1996
Third edition published 2001

ISBN 0-8020-3609-0 (cloth)
ISBN 0-8020-8461-3 (paper)

Printed on acid-free paper

National Library of Canada Cataloguing in Publication Data

Pearen, Shelley J.
  Exploring Manitoulin

  3rd ed.
  Includes index.
  ISBN 0-8020-3609-0 (bound)   ISBN 0-8020-8461-3 (pbk.)

  1. Manitoulin Island (Ont.) – History.   2. Manitoulin Island
  (Ont.) – Tours.   3. Automobile travel – Ontario – Manitoulin
  Island – Guidebooks.   I. Title.

  FC3095.M3P43 2001   971.3'135   C2001-930194-4
  F1059.M27P43 2001

University of Toronto Press acknowledges the financial assistance to
its publishing program of the Canada Council for the Arts and the
Ontario Arts Council.

University of Toronto Press acknowledges the financial support for
its publishing activities of the Government of Canada through the
Book Publishing Industry Development Program (BPIDP).

To my husband, Gordon Fulton – Aere Perennius

To my parents, Jeanne and Bayne Pearen – thank you

To my grandparents, who brought history to life

For our children, Sandy and Todd Fulton, and their generation, whose past is their key to the future

In memory of my brother Todd Sims Pearen (1960–1992), who explored Manitoulin with us for 32 years

Contents

List of Maps   viii
Preface   ix
Using This Book   xi
Introduction   xiii

1 Early Manitoulin Settlement   3
2 A Century and a Half of Touring Manitoulin   11
3 The Powwow   25
4 Manitou-miniss, the Spirit Island   31
5 Manitoulin Architecture   33
6 The La Cloche Mountains   37
7 Little Current   43
8 The Scenic North Coast (Tour 1)   57
9 The Southern Route (Tour 2)   121
10 The Eastern Bays (Tour 3)   139
11 Mindemoya Lake (Tour 4)   185
12 Around Manitou Lake (Tour 5)   197

References   213
Index   217

Maps

1 Manitoulin Island   x
2 Little Current   44
3 Little Current to Kagawong   58–9
4 Kagawong   77
5 Gore Bay   86
6 Gore Bay to Meldrum Bay   96–7
7 The Southern Route   122–3
8 The Eastern Bays   141
9 Wikwemikong   152
10 Manitowaning   160
11 Sheguiandah   172
12 Mindemoya Lake   186
13 Around Manitou Lake   198–9

Preface

The inspiration for writing this book came in July 1989, as I navigated my visiting sister-in-law, Laurie Stockton, and a life-long friend, Cheryl Mosindy, across the island from Honora Bay to Sheguiandah. As my mother and grandfather before me had always done, I gave a running commentary as we drove. About 12 km (7 miles) out on the Green Bay Road I heard myself quote my mother: 'And this is where a pioneer lime kiln was.'

'Stop here!' I yelled. I announced we were going to find this oft-described but never-viewed entity.

Within a few minutes it was discovered. Wonderful, mysterious, our secret museum was a giant pit of layers of limestone rock, charred and split by fire. As I explained the kiln's history to my guests the idea of writing an account raced through my head. By the next day, outline formed, I set to work. Having researched island history for the previous seventeen years, I found that deciding what to leave out was the hard part.

Exploring Manitoulin is a book for anyone interested in Manitoulin's past, present, or future. It is intended for both the island-born 'Haweater' who wants to learn more and the visitor who wants to discover the 'real' island. It is designed to be read before, during, or after touring, as well as by the armchair traveller who wishes to learn about the island. The book will take you from merely seeing to actually experiencing Manitoulin. Enjoy!

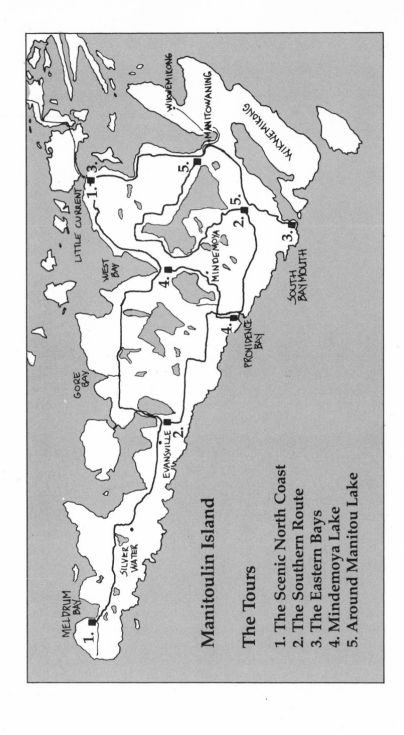

Manitoulin Island

The Tours

1. The Scenic North Coast
2. The Southern Route
3. The Eastern Bays
4. Mindemoya Lake
5. Around Manitou Lake

Using This Book

You can begin your exploration of Manitoulin with any of the tours described in this book. A good starting point would be the Little Current tour, which covers the largest town and the highway entrance to the island. The Scenic North Coast (Tour 1) takes you from Little Current, which is at the northeast corner of the island, and heads west to Meldrum Bay, the westernmost hamlet on the island. The Southern Route (Tour 2) takes you from Evansville, on the western half of the island, to South Baymouth, the seasonal ferry entrance to the island on its southeast corner.

If you are arriving by ferry at South Baymouth, you will likely want to start your tour with the Eastern Bays (Tour 3) from South Baymouth north to Little Current. Two shorter tours, Mindemoya Lake (Tour 4) and Around Manitou Lake (Tour 5), focus on the interior of the island. Tour 4 starts in West Bay and Tour 5 in Manitowaning.

Travellers arriving via Highway 6 and the Trans-Canada Highway north of the island can follow the La Cloche Mountains tour from Espanola on the mainland to Little Current.

Many of the tours can be linked to suit your tastes or time. For example, Tours 1, 2, and 3 together form a large triangle, circumnavigating the island counterclockwise from Little Current to Meldrum Bay to South Baymouth and back to Little Current.

Tours 1, 4, and 2 can be adapted to form a small square which includes Little Current, West Bay, Providence Bay, and South Baymouth.

If your island vacation is short, following all five tours in sequence may prove overwhelming. You might find your stay on Manitoulin more enjoyable if you follow one or two tours thoroughly and spend the remainder of your vacation on a beach, or fishing, or hiking, or otherwise participating in a favourite holiday activity. The aim of *Exploring Manitoulin* is, above all, to encourage visitors to take their time and savour the island.

Those who follow the tours in sequence may notice occasional repetitions from one tour to the next, where the tours overlap. This allows each tour to stand alone, for the benefit of those following only one tour per visit.

If you are travelling by bicycle remember that grocery and hardware stores are located only in the larger towns. There are two major hills for cyclists, one at West Bay and another at Ten Mile Point, both described later in this book. Follow the tours at your own pace, as did the Reverend A.P. Brace of Toronto, who made the first recorded bicycle tour of Manitoulin in the fall of 1894.

Introduction

Manitoulin, situated in Lake Huron, is the world's largest island in a freshwater lake. It is 129 km (80 miles) long, varies in width from 4 to 48 km (2.4 to 30 miles) and has more than eighty inland lakes. Its north shore forms one side of the North Channel, and its east coast, together with the Bruce Peninsula, forms Georgian Bay. Georgian Bay was originally named Lake Manitoulin by Captain William Fitzwilliam Owen, who charted the waters in 1815. It was later declared part of Lake Huron and named for King George IV by Captain Henry W. Bayfield during his survey of 1817–22.

There are two conventional approaches to Manitoulin Island. The first is from the north, by driving about 70 km (43 miles) west from Sudbury on the Trans-Canada Highway and then south on Highway 6, through Espanola. This route is noted for its high scenic passes across a rugged white quartzite ridge, the La Cloche Mountains. The other approach is by ferry, from Tobermory at the northern tip of the Bruce Peninsula, 300 km (186 miles) northwest of Toronto, landing at South Baymouth on Manitoulin Island. Residents and tourists have been arriving by this ferry route since 1932.

Manitoulin means 'Spirit Island,' based on translations of Ojibwe, Odawa, and Potawatamie languages. Manitoulin is believed to be the home of the Great Spirit, or 'Kitche Manitou.' According to Algonquin legend, Kitche Manitou created our universe as a result of a vision. He created the physical world from rock, water, fire, and wind. He then made man, or Anishnaabeg (beings made out of nothing), whom he blessed with the power of vision, like himself. The creation of Anishnaabeg is another legend in itself. The island is a rich source for wonderful and rich legends, some of which are summarized in the chapter 'Manitou-miniss, the Spirit Island.'

Manitoulin Island has a number of unusual geographical characteristics. The first serious study of the island's terrain was made in November 1862 by Public Land Surveyor John Stoughton Dennis, after the signing of a treaty which opened the island to settlement. Dennis's chief observations included the rugged north-coast cliffs surrounding deep bays and the island's southerly dip toward Lake Huron. He also described secondary cliffs running through the island, containing its lakes and rivers. Manitoulin could be described as a giant limestone formation with high bluffs along its north side sloping down to the southwest where it slides into Lake Huron. The island is part of the Niagara Escarpment, a long ridge with a steep face on one side and a gentle slope on the other. The Ontario portion of the escarpment is 700 km (435 miles) long. This ridge begins near Rochester, New York, crosses the province from Queenston on the Niagara River, extends through the Bruce Peninsula, Manitoulin Island, and St Joseph Island, and slips back into the United States. This escarpment is the visible rim of the great rock saucer known as the Michigan Basin, which partly underlies southwestern Ontario and most of Michigan.

If you drive to Manitoulin from the North Shore of Lake Huron you will travel over some of Ontario's most breathtaking terrain. The highway curves over, through, and around the beautiful massive granitic La Cloche Mountains. Then comes a dramatic contrast between two areas: the North Shore is formed of the granite and quartzite ridges of the Canadian Shield, while the island is formed of limestone, with rock plains, long perpendicular cliffs, and great inland lakes. According to Dr John Morton, co-author of *The Flora of Manitoulin*, the geologic change produces great differences in the landscape and vegetation, since limestones produce an alkaline rock, while granites and quartzite form an acidic rock. The surface of the land was moulded by the glaciers about 20,000 years ago, grinding and crushing the earth. When the glacial ice melted most of the island was covered by Lake Huron, and when the lake receded it deposited fertile silt in the valleys. A great variety of ecological niches result from the action of glaciers and water on the limestone and dolomite bedrock. The glaciers scraped across the land, creating the present landscape which alternates between flat-to-rolling farmland and rocky bush-covered hills.

As you travel, enjoy the variety of vegetation on Manitoulin Island: fringed gentians, colourful deciduous forests, various arctic species, Niagara Escarpment ferns, Manitoulin Gold Daisies, and much more. In 1865 Professor Robert Bell (1841–1917) made the first study of the island's flora. Present-day experts have recorded more than nine hundred species here (about one-fifth of Canada's total variety of plants).

Bird-watching is a popular and rewarding island activity. The Manitoulin Nature Club's booklet *Birds of Manitoulin, A Seasonal Occurrence* credits the diversity of habitats on Manitoulin both with producing 155 breeding bird species and with attracting a large variety of migrants. Try the south shore, Lake Wolsey, the escarpment cliffs, or the marshes for variety.

Fishing has attracted visitors to Manitoulin for well over one hundred years. Island 'fishing holes' range from the government docks to small inland lakes, to charter boats off the Manitoulin shores. You can also buy fresh island fish from local outlets like Cold Water Fisheries in Little Current or Purvis Brothers at Burnt Island.

Be sure to purchase copies of the island's two weekly newspapers for details on nature walks, museum programs, auctions, and Manitoulin's famous church suppers. Information on scheduled activities and accommodation is available from the Manitoulin Tourism Association, P.O. Box 119, Little Current, Ontario P0P 1K0 (705-368-3021), or from their information centre in Little Current adjacent to the swing bridge.

Exploring Manitoulin

ONE

Early Manitoulin Settlement

Anthropologists believe that North America's first people originated in Asia and migrated from Siberia across the Bering Sea. The migration occurred at least 10,000 years ago; excavations made in the past 40 years have indicated it may have occurred as long ago as 40,000 years. These first inhabitants of the glacier-covered continent were hunters. They flourished, hunting huge animals like the mammoth and the giant sloth. When the glaciers began to melt and retreat northward they remained hunters, but of smaller game.

Ontario prehistory is broken down into four periods covering 11,000 years, beginning with the Palaeo-Indian Period (9000 BC to 5000 BC) and extending to the Terminal Woodland (1000 BC to European contact). By about AD 1400 the Terminal Woodland people had evolved to the Eastern Woodlands people, who spoke languages from two unrelated linguistic families, Iroquoian and Algonquian. These were the natives the first European explorers encountered in Ontario. The Iroquois, who inhabited the temperate and fertile lands of present-day southern Ontario and northeastern United States, relied mainly on agriculture; the Algonquin, inhabiting rugged northern areas, survived by fishing and hunting. The Algonquin included Ojibwe, Montagnais, Naskapi, Micmac, Malecite, and Beothuk.

The Ojibwe are the ancestors of the majority of Manitoulin's native population. The Ojibwe included four groups: the Ojibwe of Lake Superior, the Mississauga of the Mississauga River and Manitoulin, the Odawa of Georgian Bay, and the Potawatamie of the west side of Lake Huron. The Iroquois included Erie, Huron, Neutral, Tobacco, and Five Nations Iroquois (Seneca, Cayuga, Onondaga, Oneida, and Mohawk), of whom the Huron and Five Nations Iroquois affected Manitoulin Island's history. The Iroquoian-speaking peoples had particularly strong political organizations, composed of nations which banded into confederacies. These organized and powerful people had their own confederation four hundred years before Canada's own Confederation came into existence in 1867.

The arrival of Europeans at the end of the fifteenth century had an enormous effect on all North American natives. Natives provided the Europeans with survival skills and furs; Europeans provided the natives with cloth, tools, and weapons which, eventually, drastically altered their lives and traditions. When the French explorer Samuel de Champlain (cartographer, explorer, and later governor of New France) arrived in 1603 he encountered Algonquins and their Iroquois Huron allies, who occupied the immense territory west of Lake Ontario. The Huron, or 'Wenda' (islanders) as they called themselves, were actually a confederation of four Iroquoian-speaking nations. The name Huron is based on the French term 'hure,' meaning wild boar's head, given to them for their rugged appearance and lifestyle. In 1609 Champlain helped the Algonquian Montagnais defeat the Five Nations Iroquois Mohawk, thus forming the basis of a French–Algonquin–Huron alliance. (It was an English–Five Nations Iroquois alliance which later resulted in British rule of the country.)

In addition to explorers and fur traders, France sent Roman Catholic missionaries. Champlain's aim was to establish a colony and to Christianize the natives, as well as to develop a system of trading posts. To implement his ideas, Champlain sent for Récollets and Jesuit missionaries. These priests travelled by canoe up the Ottawa River to the land of the Huron, whose population is estimated to have been twenty thousand in the year 1600. They lived among these natives, established missions, and learned their language in order to convert them to Christianity.

A commemorative plaque to one of the Jesuit missions may be seen on Manitoulin Island at Ten Mile Point. In 1648 Jesuit missionary Father Joseph Poncet was sent here to establish a mission for Algonquian-speaking natives. He was the first European resident of 'Ile-de-Ste-Marie' or 'Ekaentoton.' The exact site of Poncet's mission had not been determined.

Unfortunately, these eager European missionaries and traders spread not only the gospel and trade but European diseases. By 1640 the Huron nation had been reduced to less then half its former size, to about nine thousand people. Experts have estimated that there were about one million natives in Canada in 1500, and by 1600 their population had shrunk by 90 per cent. The original migration of the native people via the Arctic from Siberia had provided a disease barrier through extreme climate, and until the arrival of Europeans they had been sheltered from these diseases.

The Five Nations Iroquois south of the St Lawrence River feuded with all who would not join them. Warfare occurred continuously with the Hurons. By 1644 the Iroquois took advantage of the disease-reduced Huron population and began attacking. In 1650 raiding Iroquois caused Father Poncet and the Huron to abandon the Manitoulin Island mission. By 1651, according to Jesuit records, about two hundred persons in forty canoes left Manitoulin for Quebec City, where they joined a native settlement on the Ile d'Orléans. In 1652 the Iroquois attacked the Hurons' allies, driving Manitoulin Island's remaining Odawa residents west and south.

Following the Iroquois raids, Manitoulin appears to have been visited only sporadically by natives on fishing and hunting expeditions until the next permanent mission was established around 1833, at Wikwemikong. Oral tradition explains why the island was so long deserted. To cleanse the island of contagious illness, it was burned clean. It took a century or more for the vegetation and wildlife to return to their former state.

France and England competed for Canada for more than 150 years, until the Seven Years' War (1756–63) ended French rule. A British Royal Proclamation of 1763 established the borders of Quebec and the American colonies; it also defined native rights and territory, recognizing native rights to their occupied land. During the American Revolution and the War of 1812 many natives fought on the British side. Following the wars, many British allies – both native and non-native – previously living in the boundary regions of the United States resettled in Canada. In 1828 a boundary settlement between Britain and the United States prompted a further influx of natives to Manitoulin, which continued over the next few decades.

Native families began to settle at Wikwemikong around 1833, arriving from Harbor Croche, Michigan; Coldwater, Ontario; and Quebec. Many of these natives were, in a sense, returning to their homeland, as Manitoulin, or 'Ekaentoton,' had been their territory until 1650, when they fled during the Iroquois attacks. By 1839, migrating Odawa had increased Wikwemikong's population to about 350. In 1844 the Jesuits, who were then re-established in Canada, took over the Wikwemikong mission and arranged instruction in agriculture, carpentry, boatbuilding, and other trades. Wikwemikong prospered under the Jesuits, and continued migration to the peninsula caused the development of new, smaller villages such as Wikwemikongsing, Chitewaiegunning, and Buzwah.

According to the Royal Proclamation of 1763, Canadian land could not be settled until native rights were negotiated and surrendered. Twenty-four treaties were therefore signed between 1763 and 1800. Natives were gradually forced west and north from southern Ontario, pushed by the settlers and following their dwindling game. After 1812 the natives were no longer required as British military allies, and the government attempted to assimilate them into communities. In 1830 at Coldwater, near Lake Simcoe, the first assimilation experiment was attempted. The natives, however, preferred their traditional hunting and fishing lifestyle to the reserve's agriculture and industry.

In 1836 isolation, rather than assimilation, was attempted by the government. That year, Lieutenant Governor Francis Bond Head negotiated a treaty with the Odawa and Ojibwe natives on Manitoulin Island in which they agreed to 'relinquish your respective claims to the Islands [of Georgian Bay] and make them the property, under your Great Father's control, of all Indians whom he shall allow to reside on them.' Under that treaty, Manitoulin natives also agreed to allow other natives to join them. From 1836 to 1860 an 'Establishment' was organized on the island at Manitowaning, consisting of a government supported superintendent, doctor, carpenter and various mechanics, and an Anglican Church–supported clergyman, all to instruct the natives in the 'ways of civilization.' By 1843 Manitowaning contained fifty-five buildings for forty-four families. But by 1858 only twenty-two houses remained, and participation in school, workshops, and field work was decreasing. The local Indian superintendent at the time, Charles Dupont, believed the Manitowaning experiment failed principally because there was neither summer nor winter fishing at Manitowaning. The closest fishing was 7 km (4 miles) away on Manitou Lake.

The government commissioner's reports of 1858 concluded that the natives had rejected the government's supervised changes at Manitowaning, but that the Jesuit settlement at Wikwemikong was successful. He recommended the island remain as a secluded haven for natives who wished to settle there. The government felt, however, that the native population of about 1,350 did not justify their occupation of the entire island. In 1861 government representatives began negotiations to persuade the natives to cede the island and allow non-native settlement. The natives rejected the first offer of 25 acres per family plus firewood lots. In October 1862, William McDougall, superintendent general of Indian Affairs, made a second offer to the island natives, which he left for them to consider. The Wikwemikong Jesuits were known to be opposed to the treaty. When the treaty council resumed, McDougall announced that further negotiations would not include the Wikwemikong Peninsula or its people. The Jesuits were caught by surprise by this manoeuvre; the negotiators quickly obtained most of the island for settlement by agreement with representatives of less than half its population. On 6 October 1862 the Manitowaning Treaty was signed. It provided 100 acres of land for each native family, and separate provisions for single persons and orphans. Each native was permitted to select a lot, provided the native lots were adjacent and formed compact native settlements, and water lots were not future mill sites or village park lots. The interest from the proceeds of land sales, less government expenses, was to be divided among the natives annually.

Dupont was assigned the task of establishing native lots or reserves. Despite dogged efforts, he was unable to settle the reserve location question before non-native settlement began officially in June 1866 – most natives favoured remaining where they were before the treaty. By 1867 the location of the Manitowaning reserve had become so controversial that a local missionary, Jabez Sims, who two years earlier had named his fifth son after the superintendent, publicly accused Dupont of personally coveting the land. Dupont called Sims 'a brazen-faced liar' three times, then hit Sims hard on the face, drawing blood, saying 'I can afford to pay for striking a clergyman.' Over the next year the remaining Manitowaning natives (and Sims) migrated to Sheguiandah, and a few relocated to Sucker Lake. Superintendent Dupont was replaced by William Plummer, who finally resolved the reserve location problems. Over the next decade the Sheguiandah, West Bay (now M'Chigeeng), and Shesheguaning reserves were established at existing native villages; Sucker Lake reserve was created for some of the Manitowaning natives; Cockburn Island reserve, for some of the Shesheguaning natives; Sucker Creek reserve, for the Little Current natives; and Obidjiwang reserve, for non-Christian natives formerly from Gore Bay and the island's west end.

The first Manitoulin land was offered for sale in June 1866, though enthusiastic settlers had already begun to arrive two years earlier. To encourage settlement a road was started from Little Current to Sheguiandah, extended to Manitowaning by 1871, and finally completed to Michael's Bay. But initial sales were slow, and by 1871 fewer than 35,000 acres had been sold. By the mid-1870s land sales were finally booming. By 1874 non-native settlements were established at the former native camps of Kagawong, Gore Bay, Providence Bay, and Michael's Bay, as well as the original settlements of Little Current and Manitowaning. Many of the townships were organized into municipalities and public buildings were built.

The earliest settlers typically arrived in small groups of relatives. Most were of similar background and nationality: many were English, Irish, or Scottish Protestants from the nearby counties of southern Ontario, people whose parents had emigrated from Great Britain a few decades earlier. Most came to establish their own homesteads and a future for their children. They produced modest buildings, initially rough log structures which evolved over decades to larger farm homes and barns.

The first land sales were near and between the main steamer port of Little Current and the land office at Manitowaning. Land was sold for fifty cents an acre cash, to a maximum of 200 acres. The new owner had to occupy the land within six months and could obtain a patent after residing there for three years and clearing 10 of the 200 acres. By June 1867 these terms were loosened to encourage sales: twenty cents per acre, with a maximum of 400 acres. Naturally, the accessible eastern portion of the island sold first, followed by the central portion in the mid-1870s, and lastly the west end of the island. The west was sold under different terms: the lots were valued according to agricultural potential, ranging from twenty cents to one dollar per acre, and an instalment plan was used.

TWO

A Century and a Half of Touring Manitoulin

Exploring Manitoulin is not a recent phenomenon: the island has been a popular destination for more than 160 years. The first 'tourist' was Mrs Anna Brownell Jameson, who visited Manitowaning in 1837. Others had visited before, but for religious, trade, or government purposes. Mrs Jameson was an Irish-born writer and the wife of Upper Canada's attorney general Robert Sympson Jameson. She travelled from York (Toronto) to Chatham, then by steamboat to Detroit and Mackinac Island, by bateau to Manitoulin, and by canoe to Penetanguishene. Her adventures were published as *Winter Studies and Summer Rambles in Canada*.

When she arrived at Manitowaning, 3,700 'Ottawas, Chippewas, Pottowattomies, Winnebagoes, and Menomonies' were assembled to receive their annual gifts from the government. She attended the grand council of chiefs, a women's canoe race, and a war dance – and witnessed the construction of a canoe:

> In walking among the wigwams today, I found some women on the shore, making a canoe. The frame had been put together by the men. The women were then joining the pieces of birchbark, with the split ligaments of the pine root, called wattop. Other

women were employed in melting and applying the resinous gum, with which they smear the seams, and render them impervious to the water. There was much chattering and laughing meanwhile, and I never saw a merrier set of gossips. This canoe, which was about eighteen feet in length, was finished before night; and the next morning I saw it afloat.

The annual gift ceremony attracted artist Paul Kane in 1845. He spent two weeks studying and sketching the natives. At Manitowaning he found 'nearly 2000 Indians, waiting the arrival of the vessel that was freighted with their annual presents, comprising guns, ammunition, axes, kettles and implements useful to the Indian.' He later published *Wanderings of an artist among the Indians of North America, from Canada to Vancouver's Island and Oregon through the Hudson's Bay Companies territory and back again.*

By 1850, the steamboat *Gore* was carrying passengers and freight between Georgian Bay ports and Sault Ste Marie via Manitoulin. In 1853, it was replaced by the 188-foot sidewheeler *Kaloolah*. British author William H.G. Kingston and his bride travelled on this steamer, 'a huge, white, unsubstantial looking construction,' in the fall of 1853. They occupied the only stateroom. Other berths were laid along the side of the saloon and in the ladies' cabin. Kingston published his travels as *Western Wanderings or, a Pleasure Tour in the Canadas*, in 1856.

Laurence Oliphant attended the annual distribution of presents at Manitowaning in 1854, and visited 'Petit Courant, a small village inhabited by Indians who gain their livelihood by supplying steamers with wood. We landed on Sunday, and attended service in an Indian's log house.' He later published *Minnesota and the Far West*, in which he described his fellow steamboat passengers as 'emigrants from Europe, speculators from the States, tourists from all parts of the world, rough backwoodsmen and mysterious characters journeying towards the limits of civilisation, for reasons best known to themselves.' He remarked that 'the whole passenger accommodation is upon deck. Sometimes there are cabins opening off the saloons; but in the boat we were in, the berths were screened off simply by curtains suspended to bars.'

In 1855, the Ontario, Simcoe, and Huron Railway, or 'Northern Railway,' reached Collingwood. The steamboat business rapidly expanded to serve the traffic of freight, mail, tourists, labourers, and immigrants. Two years later, John Disturnell published *A Trip Through the Lakes of North America*. He described 'a new and highly interesting steamboat excursion commencing with a 94-mile railroad trip, from Toronto to Collingwood, where great numbers of travellers and emigrants, are transferred to magnificent steamers bound for Mackinac, Green Bay, Chicago and the Great West as well as to Sault Ste Marie and Lake Superior. From Collingwood, a 36-hour scenic steamboat cruise terminated at Soo, Michigan. The steamboat costs $8.50 including meals.' At Little Current he reported 'Indians are often seen here in considerable numbers. They are reported to be indolent and harmless.'

The 1860s were years of drastic change on Manitoulin. In 1862 the majority of the island was ceded to the government for non-native settlement. Surveyors began dividing the island into townships. Mid-decade saw a brief oil speculation boom, and in June 1866 the first Manitoulin land was sold. This flurry of activity brought visitors with specific purposes in mind: exploration, settlement, commerce, and speculation. Many visitors were given tours by local residents. In 1865, a Mr Cail from Goderich, Ontario, toured and left with souvenirs of a box of bark-work and a pincushion of Indian beadwork.

From 1864 through 1873, the three-masted sidewheeler *Algoma* called regularly at Little Current. The $10.00 fare from Owen Sound to Sault Ste Marie included meals and a berth. The temperament of Georgian Bay, however, determined whether a passenger could enjoy these amenities. Typically, the *Algoma* departed Collingwood late at night and reached Little Current about 30 hours later. Manitoulin residents anxiously awaited the safe arrival of the boat. On 28 November 1864, the Algoma's late arrival prompted one islander to record 'our fears are now put to rest; the *Algoma* has returned.' The Algoma's competition included the *Stanley*, the *Waubano* from 1867, and the *Chicora* from 1869.

In 1870, Bryan Mackie built a hotel in Little Current and John Cole received permission from the Indian Department to erect a house in Manitowaning 'for accommodation of the public provided no spirituous liquors of any kind be kept by him.'

Modes of travel continued to improve. In *Across Georgian Bay in 1871*, J.H. Coyne described a comfortable and interesting voyage. At Collingwood he boarded the 235-foot steamboat *Chicora*, which 'rode the waves beautifully' except 'in open water [when] some fellow passengers were unable to enjoy their tea.' The *Chicora* was carrying 65 passengers, of whom at least 50 were making the round trip. The passengers included a Member of the Provincial Parliament, a New York gentleman who attempted to purchase the boat, a Scotsman, lawyers, merchants, and families seeking to escape the heat of midsummer. Little Current was described then as an Indian village, with a portion of its population living in birchbark wigwams. Coyne was particularly interested in a store near the wharf, where 'great quantities of Indian work, such as canoes and boxes made of birchbark and adorned with porcupine quills, baskets and mats made of grass etc. are sold to passengers on steamers.' Although romantic descriptions of native villages with wigwams may have promoted Manitoulin tourism, most residents at this time – including the natives – resided in log cabins, and the settlement of Little Current contained four stores with wharves, a hotel, and a log church.

In the summer of 1874, Canada's Governor General, the Marquess of Dufferin and Ava, spent two weeks with his wife, Hariot, touring the Upper Great Lakes aboard the steamboat *Chicora*. At Manitoulin they were greeted by a group of self-described 'hungry' natives, to whom the vice-regal couple donated a barrel of flour and a hundred-weight of pork.

By 1874, the Lake Superior Royal Mail Line and the Northern Railway were operating three first-class sidewheel steamboats, the *Chicora*, the *Cumberland*, and the *Frances Smith*.

From its inception in 1879, the *Manitoulin Expositor* newspaper regularly featured articles proclaiming Manitoulin as a summer resort for 'anglers rods, beautiful natural scenery, boating and bathing.'

A delightful trip of 20 hours by steamer from Collingwood to Killarney; then a short run to Manitowaning the course being thickly studded with beautiful islands while away to the north the towering mountains on the North Shore rise grandly into view and form a fitting boundary to the view in that direction. At Manitowaning they find a thriving village with magnificent bay for boating and bathing, fishing and natural scenery abounds, also run over to the Indian village of Wequiemekong with its 800 inhabitants and church buildings. A 25 mile run to Little Current with innumerable channels to explore and picnic at, first class accommodation at Queens Hotel. Also can make their way by easy stages to the Sault. Those who have already made the trip consider the scenery between Killarney and the Sault equal if not superior to anything on the St Lawrence and we feel certain that anyone who may make the trip will have no reason to regret the money and time spent in doing so.

Travel, although increasingly comfortable, was not without risk. In November 1879 the steamer *Waubano*, which had served Georgian Bay ports for more than a decade, disappeared under the waves. The *Waubano* was replaced by the *Manitoulin*, which caught fire in May 1882 four miles from Manitowaning. The burning boat was driven at a full throttle towards the shore and beached, but eleven persons who panicked and jumped ship were drowned. The *Manitoulin*'s replacement, the *Asia*, sank just four months later. Only two of her 200 passengers survived.

The Saunders family visited Manitoulin in 1880. William Edwin Saunders recorded the highlights in his journal: 'Little Current's two nice hotels, quite a number of houses and a few Indian wigwams 1/2 mile to the east; Gore Bay's lockup – a gigantic building, the lighthouse and the Ocean House Hotel.'

The number of visitors to the island continued to increase during the 1880s. Sightseeing, fishing, and hunting were very popular activities. In 1880 Manitoulin had nine licensed hotels, two each at Gore Bay, Little Current, Sheguiandah, and Manitowaning, and one at Michael's Bay. Providence Bay and Kagawong soon had hotels too.

Some visitors became summer residents, returning annually on the steamboats or their own yachts. By 1878, a Captain Bell had established a sumer residence on Barrie Island. Two years later, 'rustic houses' were built on Strawberry Island for Peter Gow and his brother-in-law Robert Melvin of Guelph, Ontario.

Gow was the sheriff of Wellington County, Ontario. His 1886 obituary noted that Manitoulin's 'invigorating air did much to resuscitate his failing health.' Another Guelph resident, A.R. Petrie, purchased Isle of Beauty in 1882, where he built a summer residence four years later. The following year, a Toronto deputy chief of police, William McPherson, purchased Mindemoya or Treasure Island. Islands were popular, but so were lakeshore properties. In 1884, J.N. Smith was reported to be erecting a summer house on Gore Bay's east range.

In 1883, Great Northern Transit advertised two large new steamboats, the *Atlantic* and the *Pacific*: 'These steamers are new and built expressly for the route and are second to none in Canada for combined speed, strength and comfort. They depart Collingwood twice weekly for Killarney, Manitowaning, Little Current, Kagawong, Gore Bay, and north shore ports to Sault Ste Marie.' The boats' captains were also touted for their safety, speed, or feats of daring they had performed.

The local papers publicized tourists' adventures. In 1883, they reported on a party of Guelph sportsmen who spent a week fishing on the Manitou River after reading a favourable article in *Forest and Stream* magazine. An article in 1886 described Ed Whalen of Buffalo, who had arrived on the steamboat *Atlantic* for his fifth annual fishing expedition. In 1888, 'a party of four caught 500 trout in the Blue Jay Creek.'

Pleasure yachts regularly visited island waters. The P.J. Perrott family from Bay City, Michigan, visited annually on their 57-foot yacht *Julia*. Perrott's family had fished the Manitoulin waters commercially in the 1860s.

Hunting was popular. In 1884, the *Manitoulin Expositor* announced that sportsmen could now find red deer at Michael's Bay and Providence Bay, 'where six years ago none existed.' Ducks, partridges, and passenger pigeons were also popular targets.

More travel guides were published, including *The Northern Lakes of Canada Guidebook* in 1886. It explained to potential tourists that 'first class express trains depart Toronto for Collingwood on Georgian Bay, to connect with splendid steamers of the Great Northern Transit Company for Manitoulin Island, Sault Ste Marie, etc.' The book briefly described the island's steamer

'There were so many we thought they would never run out,' commented one of these hunters who 'treated the town to a dinner of Black Ducks, Whistlers, Mallards, Butterballs, Bluebills and Mergansers.'

stops, and typically commented on amenities such as Manitowaning's 'good trout streams and two hotels.'

In June 1886, the steamer *Frances Smith* made a specially advertised excursion to Manitoulin. Visitors were invited to the Corpus Christi festival at Wikwemikong, the new Pike Lake oil wells site, Fossil Hill, Ten Mile Point, Lake Manitou, and even a lacrosse match between 'the Manitowaning club and the Cape Croker Indians.' The round-trip fare was $2.00, plus the cost of meals and a stateroom.

Optimists predicted Manitoulin would become Ontario's most popular camping area. More than 60 watercraft were moored in Little Current harbour for the 1 July celebration in 1890.

During the 1890s, competition increased between the steamboat companies operating coasters, or lineboats. The North Shore Navigation Company, identified by their black-painted boats, ran the *City of London, City of Collingwood, City of Midland,*

City of Toronto, and *City of Parry Sound* steamboats from Owen Sound and Collingwood to Sault Ste Marie and Mackinac, where they connected with United States steamers to Chicago. The Great Northern Transit Company (white-painted boats), in conjunction with the Grand Trunk Railway, operated the *Pacific, Atlantic, Baltic, Northern Belle, Majestic*, and *Germanic*. This competition ended when North Shore Navigation bought out Great Northern, forming the Northern Navigation Company and the Northwest Transportation Company in 1899.

Other competition included the Canada Transit Company, with the CPR sidewheelers *Carmona* and *Cambria*; the Algoma Central Steamship Line's *Ossifrage, Minnie M*, and *King Edward*; the Algoma Navigation Company's *City of Owen Sound* and *City of Windsor*; and Georgian Bay Navigation's *Pittsburgh*. In 1900, it was common to see half a dozen large steamboats moored in Little Current or Gore Bay harbours, plus a constant stream of tugboats with log booms.

Hotels expanded and improved. In Little Current, Jehiel Tinkis's Mansion House Hotel (now the Anchor Inn) opened in 1888 with a claim to be the finest accommodation in the region. H.B. Hunt's Hotel Manitoulin in Gore Bay opened in 1892. It was built at a cost of $8,000, and could accommodate 100 guests. John Hilliard opened his new Havelock Hotel in Kagawong in 1896. This 15-room hotel was famous for its convenient location to smallmouth bass fishing.

In 1906, the *South Atlantic Quarterly* published 'On Manitoulin,' by Bernard C. Steiner.

> We touched at Manitowaning. There we had pointed out in the distance the Jesuit Mission of 'Wickwemiquong,' where the fathers still teach the Hurons, as they did in the country farther south, before the Iroquois drove them away and Strawberry Island where looking past its lighthouse we saw the spire of a church and below it three tall iron smokestacks; that is the Roman Catholic church served by the 'Wickwemiquong' priest and the Picnic Mill stacks. We stop at the wharf at the east end of Little Current. It is a picturesque view which meets our eyes when we have climbed to the west end of Robinson St. The narrows cause the waters to run with the rapid current, whence the town takes its name. The hills of the

The *SS Caribou* carried passengers, freight, mail, and automobiles.

North Shore rise in the distance. Nearer are the barren shores of La Cloche Island, the flat and stony acres of Goat Island, the higher and wooded land of Beauty Island, tiny Spider Islet in the west and Picnic and Mill islands whose names bear record to departed pleasure and industry. In its heyday there were five sawmills here. Little Current does have a present and a future – the grazing industry is sure to increase, and log booms pass through here, the universal board sidewalk leads to a new race track for horses and a railway is proposed. Manitoulin Island is cut off in winter, except for telegraph cable; the mail carrier crosses the ice by sled, and when the ice is heavy, the stage is sent forth, covered with painted canvas and adorned with advertisements, just like a city omnibus. This vehicle on runners makes the trip in three or four hours.

By 1906 Dominion Transportation was operating two local boat routes. Their Georgian Bay division ran the *SS Caribou* and *SS Manitou* between Owen Sound and Sault Ste Marie, with stops at Killarney, Manitowaning, Little Current, Gore Bay, Meldrum

Bay, Cockburn Island, and several North Shore ports, plus Kagawong on the return trip. Their Manitoulin Island Route, which ran the steamer *SS Telegram*, visited Tobermory, Fitz William, South Baymouth, Providence Bay, and the Duck Islands.

When the Algoma Eastern Railway reached Little Current in 1913 via a new railway bridge, Manitoulin was no longer entirely dependent on boats. Though it was not obvious at the time, the bridge connection was the beginning of the end for the North Shore lineboats.

The Owen Sound Transportation Company was formed in 1921, and the decade that followed put the steamships *SS Michipicoten*, *SS Manasoo*, and *SS Manitoulin* on an Owen Sound–Manitoulin–Sault Ste Marie run. These ships slept 100 passengers, had comfortable dining facilities, and carried 200 tons of freight. Soon, automobiles were being carried on the boats.

Automobiles enhanced and expanded tourism. Camping parks, restaurants, tourist camps, and private homes all over Manitoulin welcomed tourists. Many visitors extended their Manitoulin visit from brief stops at Manitoulin ports to automobile tours of island highlights. In June 1921, Canada's governor general, the Duke of Devonshire, and the Marquess and Marchioness of Hartington arrived on James Playfair's luxury yacht *Pathfinder*. They then travelled by automobile to several island highlights, including Ten Mile Point Lookout. In August 1924, the lieutenant governor of Ontario, Henry (Harry) Cockshutt, toured the island extensively, visiting Alex Purvis's Burnt Island fish station. By 1924 a rough road even reached Meldrum Bay at the island's western extremity.

An article written in 1923 by Little Current resident T.J. Pattern for the Algonquin Historical Society reported that 'a wagon road is now being built, by the Ontario Government, from the Great Northern Colonization road which will connect the Manitoulin, at Little Current, with, we might say, the rest of North America for motor car travel. There are magnificent motor car roads all over the Manitoulin Island, thanks to a considerate government, and it is fast becoming a great resort for motorists.'

The highway from the North Shore finally reached La Cloche in 1929. From there, a small ferry delivered autos to Little Current. The local paper covered the first car's trip:

Billie Sims (1894–1985), the author's grandfather, exploring Manitoulin in his Model T Ford.

On Aug 12 Mr. Jaffary, of Gore Bay, driving a new 1929 Ford Coupe, accompanied by Harry Campbell of Little Current travelled across the channel by scow, then on ungravelled road from La Cloche to Birch Island where it was described as fairly hard going, but from then on good roads. The road was rather narrow with many sharp bends and steep inclines but, for the careful motorist a safe, beautiful drive as the mountainous nature of the country offers many beautiful views typical of the North Country.

Three years later, drivers were demanding a better road north. Local newspaper editor E.C. Davis complained 'our rough highway from the north, with its hairpin turns, dips and gullies, probably induced as much seasickness as the *Normac* ferry.' He proclaimed it the 'Highway Roller Coaster of the North.' Most travellers agreed, after following its 'five hundred scenic curves.'
By the summer of 1931 the Owen Sound Transportation Com-

pany's 90-foot steamboat *Kagawong* was making a daily run between Tobermory and South Baymouth. In 1932, the company was granted the exclusive government franchise to run a ferry between South Baymouth and Tobermory. The first ferry was the 13-car *Normac*. For several years, ferry competition continued in the water and in the courts, as John Tackaberry's Blue Water Transportation Company fought to secure the franchise for its boat, *Islet Prince*. The Owen Sound Transportation Company and Dominion Transportation Company were combined, continuing as the OSTCo. The *SS Manitoulin* and *SS Manitou* were their passenger and freight ships, and the *MS Normac* and *SS Caribou* did the South Baymouth ferry run. The regular ferry run provided the incentive for Clara and George Britten to open the Huron Motor Lodge in 1932. They provided a night's accommodation and three meals a day for $2.50.

During the 1930s, yachting, deer hunting, fishing, and visiting John R. Miller's rock garden on Lake Mindemoya were popular tourist activities. By mid-decade, cruise ships such as the four-deck *Georgian* from Detroit were bringing tourists to Manitoulin. In 1938, the Manitoulin Camp Owners Association and the Manitoulin Chamber of Commerce were formed. The island's inspector of schools and the agricultural representative offered a winter course called 'Catering for Tourists.' Members of the Women's Institute instructed and taught women aged 18 to 30 in hospitality, etiquette, and culinary skills. A yachting column in the *Manitoulin Expositor* noted 71 yachts moored in Little Current harbour one July day in 1931.

Ferry traffic was regularly announced in the local papers. A new record for the Little Current ferry was set on 28 July 1940, when it carried 519 cars and more than 1,500 passengers. In the summer of 1940 visitors from southern Ontario had a choice of five daily ferry trips on the *SS Manitou* (a steam ship) or *MS Normac* (a motor ship, or diesel).

As automobile touring increased in popularity the island's resorts developed to accommodate these new tourists. A 1940 'Where to go on Manitoulin Island' brochure claimed that 'five hundred miles of first class roads, running by lake shores and through miles of forests, provide the summer visitor with easy access to all the leading fishing and hunting grounds, camping

A tourist's transportation and accommodation about 1940.

grounds and bathing beaches.' More than 50 resorts and six hotels were listed, including Hunt's Havelock Hotel, Hodgson's Treasure Island, George Bishop's Red Lodge, Bass Creek (room and board $2.50 per day), Captain W.R. Cummins Manitowaning Lodge ($25.00 per week with meals), W.M. Sanderson's Silver Birches, and the Huron Lodge.

In 1945, the 1913 railway bridge at Little Current was converted to accommodate automobiles as well as trains. Rapidly improving highways decreased the need for passenger and freight ships, but increased the demand for ferry service. In 1946–7 the steamer *SS Caribou* was replaced by the new 'all steel, modern, fireproof' *SS Norisle*. The *Norisle* promoted an enjoyable three-hour boat cruise and the shortest route to Manitoulin Island – thus saving gas and time. Automobiles travelled for $3.00. Full-course meals were available, as were stateroom berths for the crossing or overnight.

In 1946, the Hon. E. Ray Lawson, lieutenant-governor of Ontario, visited with his family. They arrived in Little Current by railway car and toured the town. The arrival of celebrities by yacht was announced in the local papers. Lana Turner and Gene Autry visited in 1949–50.

North Shore lineboat traffic continued to decline. In 1950 the new *SS Norgoma* replaced the aging *SS Manitoulin*. The *Norgoma* could carry 200 passengers and 200 tons of freight. From 1950 through 1963, the *Norgoma* made the Owen Sound–North Shore–Manitoulin trip for the Owen Sound Transportation Company. In 1964, the *Norgoma* was transferred to assist on the popular Tobermory to South Baymouth run. The western end of Manitoulin was also served by a ferry: the *MS Normac* operated between Meldrum Bay and Blind River until 1968. In 1964 it ran this two-hour trip twice daily, in addition to a weekly service to Cockburn Island.

In 1959, Edward Dreier, an American tourist, and W.J. Patterson, the publisher of the *Manitoulin Expositor*, co-published an important tourist information booklet entitled *This is Manitoulin*. By 1964 it had grown to a forty-page issue describing in detail Manitoulin's highlights, accommodation, and services, listing more than 75 motel or cottage businesses, ten camping parks, and hundreds of local services. This publication has been continued by the *Manitoulin Expositor*, and today remains an excellent reference for visitors.

While the North Shore lineboat traffic declined, the southern ferry route continued to grow. In 1964 the former North Shore boat *Norgoma* was converted to diesel power and joined the *Norisle* on the South Baymouth ferry run. But their combined capacity of 400 passengers and more than 80 autos was still not enough. The provincial government's Ontario Northland Transportation Company bought Owen Sound Transportation in 1974, and the *MS Chi-Cheemaun* (Big Canoe) was built for the South Baymouth route. The *Norgoma* and the *Norisle* were retired. The latter, the last coal-fired steamer on the Great Lakes, can now be visited at the Manitowaning wharf. The *Chi-Cheemaun* has a capacity of 143 vehicles and more than 600 passengers. From 1989 until 1993 the *MS Nindawayma* assisted on this route.

Visitors and residents in the twenty-first century explore most of the same unique attractions that visitors have enjoyed for more than a century and a half. The island's untamed Niagara Escarpment cliffs and its waterfalls, wildlife, native culture, boating, and unrivalled exploring continue to attract and entertain.

THREE

The Powwow

According to the *Gage Canadian Dictionary*, a powwow is, 'among North American Indian peoples, a celebration or ceremony, usually featuring feasting and dancing and certain rites, held before an expedition, hunt, council, or conference.' A powwow is the rhythmic pounding of a drum, the sounds of unified voices singing and feet striking the earth, a swirling rainbow of colour, the scents of campfires, cedar, sawdust, and sweet grass.

The powwow experience is being rediscovered by both natives and non-natives. It is a truly mesmerizing event that all visitors to Manitoulin should make time to attend. To visit a powwow is to participate in native culture, a spiritual experience that can be the highlight of many vacations.

Manitoulin Island is a natural host for powwows. The traditional Algonquian name for Manitoulin, Manitou-miniss, or Spirit Island, still accurately describes this unique isle. The 1990s saw a resurgence of Spirit or Manitou here. The most visible sign of this spiritual revival is the powwow, although native arts, crafts, and theatre have also enjoyed a renaissance.

About half of Manitoulin's population of 10,000 are native Canadians. Most reside on the island's six First Nations. All of these communities hold summer powwows that visitors are welcome to attend.

Powwows have probably been held since the beginning of time. They have been recorded on Manitoulin since at least the 1830s, although they were often described as war dances or festivals. They usually followed gatherings such as the annual presentation of gifts to the natives or New Year and Christmas celebrations, and consisted of dancing, singing, and feasting. The island's powwows almost disappeared in the early part of the twentieth century, but were revived at Wikwemikong in 1961. Rosemary (Peltier) Odjig-Fisher spearheaded an effort to hold a traditional song and dance or 'Indian Dance Festival' similar to ones she and her siblings had visited in western Canada. She believed the powwow could help preserve and revive native culture, language, and traditions. She was correct, and thanks to her efforts and those of many members of the Wikwemikong community the powwow is now a vital part of Manitoulin culture.

Most powwows are held in a large multi-purpose clearing, often the community baseball diamond, which is magically transformed with natural decoration. At the centre is a large cedar-covered arbour to shelter the drummers. It is surrounded by a large circular sawdust-covered parade ground. Smaller arbours may be set off to the side to shelter elders and dancers. A master of ceremonies provides history and information.

Traditionally a weekend event, the powwow usually opens at 1:00 pm on Saturday with a grand entry procession. The procession arrives from the east, the direction signifying the beginning of life. It is led by those who have earned the right, typically a veteran or the owner of an eagle staff, the ancient emblem of courage. They are followed by the male and female lead dancers, and then by all the other participants.

A song in honour of veterans and/or other nations present is 'sung.' The song is actually a rhythmic pounding of many sticks on a lone drum, accompanied by the haunting song of unified voices. Listen to the drum. It is not background, but the heartbeat and lifeblood of the powwow. Drummers sit in groups around a large communal drum. There may be as many as a dozen drum groups, but at the very least there are two, a host and a guest drum group. The drummers play many different songs, including honour songs, flag songs, veteran songs, contest songs, and intertribal songs.

A bilingual (Ojibwe and English) invocation is given, followed by greetings from the Chief and the master of ceremonies, and then an invitation to dance. An opening ceremony is usually held twice on Saturday (at 1:00 pm and 7:00 pm) and at noon or 1:00 pm on Sunday. Dances alternate between exhibition, competitive, and intertribal dances. Everyone is encouraged to dance during intertribal dances. The dances range from traditional earth- and animal-based styles to spellbinding hoop dances, and the fancy dance with elaborate jumps. At competitive powwows cash prizes may be awarded for women's jingle dress, women's and junior women's traditional, women's and girl's shawl, men's and boy's grass, men's fancy, women's and men's golden age, and family dances.

Costumes are as important as the dances. Traditional outfits feature bear-claw necklaces, animal headpieces, and eagle feathers. The jingle or healing dresses jingle with dangling metal cones. The cones are formed by wrapping metal around a cedar bough. This is thought to instill the cedar's healing power into the cone and thus to the woman wearing the dress.

The judges examine dancing talent and costumes. They observe rhythm, timing, and footwork, and costume detail and construction.

Numerous craft and food booths circle the grounds. Artists display and sell traditional native crafts such as sweet grass braids, porcupine quill decoration on birchbark boxes, and beadwork on deer skin. A variety of food is available, often including fried bannock, corn soup, and moose burgers.

Manitoulin's Powwow Sites

Wikwemikong, the first settlement on the island to revive the powwow, has held one since 1961 on the early August long weekend. It is by far the largest powwow on Manitoulin. About 500 dancers and many drum groups from all over North America compete for thousands of dollars in prizes. The objective of the Wikwemikong Heritage Organization is to preserve Anishinabe songs, stories, and dances. A visit to the powwow confirms their success not only in preserving their culture but in

A traditional male dancer at the Sheguiandah Powwow.

sharing it with natives and non-natives alike. A local art show and theatre production are held in conjunction with the pow-wow. Although the powwow attracts thousands, the large site handles the crowds capably as people wander between specta-tor bleachers and dozens of food and craft booths.

Since 1988, the M'Chigeeng (West Bay) First Nation has held a traditional powwow in celebration of youth and culture. A tra-ditional powwow's emphasis is on participation and education rather than the competitive powwow's judging and prizes. This powwow is situated below M'Chigeeng or West Bay's bluffs, an Ojibwe spiritual place. This event, the island's second largest powwow, is usually held on Labour Day weekend in early Sep-tember.

Since 1990 Sheguiandah First Nation has also held a tradi-tional powwow. Its location among the trees between Sheguian-dah Bay and the community's historic Anglican church is the island's most picturesque powwow site. This community-based event is held annually in early July.

Sucker Creek First Nation also began holding a traditional powwow in 1990. It is held in June, and is opened by a sunrise pipe ceremony and sacred fire lighting. This community's emphasis is also on participation and youth.

Some of the smaller First Nations have recently begun their own powwows. Sheshegwaning on western Manitoulin held its first annual powwow in 1994. Zhiibaahaasing, formerly known as Cockburn Island First Nation, holds a powwow in early July. This tiny community contains the world's largest dream catcher and peace pipe. Buzwah, on the Wikwemikong Peninsula, holds a traditional powwow every June. Nearby, on the La Cloche Peninsula, the Wawaskinaga or Whitefish River First Nation has held a powwow since 1994, at Sunshine Alley beneath Dreamer's Rock, a historic and sacred site.

A powwow is a wonderful introduction to First Nation cul-ture. Remember your camera and take lots of film, sunscreen, and a hat. Admission is usually by a very reasonable donation. Further information on dates and accommodation can be obtained from the Manitoulin Tourism Association, P.O. Box 119, Little Current, Ontario P0P 1K0 (705) 368-3021.

FOUR

Manitou-miniss, the Spirit Island

The word Manitoulin means 'Spirit Island,' based on translations of Ojibwe, Odawa, and Potawatamie languages. Manitoulin is believed to be the home of the Great Spirit, or Kitche
Manitou. The Algonquian-speaking peoples tell similar versions of the story of the Creation. (On this subject, books by
Basil Johnston beautifully re-create the traditional legends.) The
story of the Creation and Great Flood became lore in my own
family in 1865 when Peter Ahwunagwud of Manitowaning
related the story to my great-great-grandfather Jabez W. Sims,
an Anglican missionary. Here is the Creation:

> Kitche Manitou (The Great Spirit) had a vision of the universe. He
> meditated to understand his vision, and realized his task was to
> fulfil the vision by creating the world that he had dreamed. He
> began by making rock, water, fire, and wind, and from these he
> created the physical world of the stars and planets. On earth he
> detailed landforms and waters, then plants and animals, all of
> which were blessed with special gifts, such as healing. Then he
> made man, upon whom he bestowed his greatest gift, the power
> to dream. All were to use their gifts to live together in peace.
>
> But peace did not last; rain created a great flood, drowning the
> people, plants, and land animals. Eventually the rain ceased. The

earth was covered by water. The spirit Sky-Woman descended from the sky and settled on a turtle's back. She sent all the animals in search of land. The muskrat was finally successful, retrieving soil from the water's bottom to create the Island of Michilimackinac, or Place of the Great Turtle's Back.

Then the spirit Sky-Woman asked Kitche Manitou for a companion in order to bear children. She bore twins, a male and a female. The male, like Kitche Manitou, was blessed with the power of vision, and the female with the power to give life. The new children were called 'Anishnaabeg,' or 'beings made out of nothing.' Sky-Woman raised her children and then returned to the heavens, eventually to be joined by her children. She is symbolized by the moon, while Kitche Manitou is symbolized by the sun.

Later, Nanabush was sent to the world by Kitche Manitou to teach the Anishnaabeg. Nanabush was born of a human mother and spirit father, but was raised by his grandmother. He possessed supernatural powers, such as the power of transformation, and was a spirit in nature as well as a trickster. Both Nanabush and his grandmother are the basis of numerous local legends, including the formation of Mindemoya Lake Island and Cup and Saucer Hill.

Other legends describe the formation of Manitoulin itself. When Kitche Manitou created the world he set aside the best of each piece of Creation: the bluest, most sparkling water; the whitest, most fleecy clouds; the brightest stars; the most fertile fields; the greenest forests. When he was finished the earth he created from these special pieces an island and set it in an inland sea, Lake Huron, where it drifted to the North Shore's rugged coast. He was pleased with this setting of extreme contrast, the North Shore's rough coast against the delicate island. He secured the island in place and proclaimed it 'Manitou-miniss' or Island of Manitou.

In M'Chigeeng, at the Ojibwe Cultural Foundation, you may purchase a series of legend booklets. These beautifully written and illustrated stories are a delight for young and old.

FIVE

Manitoulin Architecture

The first settlers' homes were built of logs. There were plenty of trees to be cleared and a log home, whether of round or squared logs, could be constructed quickly. The logs were usually peeled, as unpeeled logs held vermin and could catch fire when their bark dried out. Peeling the logs also made them easier to chink (fill the spaces in between) with a mixture of hay and daub or with mortar. Sometimes the logs were covered with lath and plaster for insulation and aesthetics. As soon as time and money allowed, the settlers erected wood frame homes, and the original log house often became an outbuilding.

The first log homes were usually one storey high; wood frame homes were usually one-and-a-half storeys high. These typical heights developed in Ontario early in the nineteenth century because of the taxation system, whereby houses of two or more storeys were taxed at a higher rate. Settlers increased the height of the ground floor walls of a rectangular shaped house and put the door on the long side. The roof gables containing the second storey's windows were on the short side, creating a house that from the front appeared to be a tall single storey. Thus a settler had the floor area of a two-storey home – though with a sloping ceiling on the second floor – but paid taxes for only one storey. By 1870 this most common house form had evolved to contain a small gable window over the front door to allow more light into the upper storey.

In style, the houses were similar to those the pioneers had left behind in southern Ontario, modest with a minimum of architectural detail. Three basic styles of farmhouse can be recognized on Manitoulin Island. Two are based on a rectangular floor plan; the third, on a square plan.

The first, the 'Centre Hall' or 'Centre Gable' (photo p. 100), is symmetrically planned with the front façade on the long side. The door, which is usually in the middle of the front façade, often has a centre gable over it, and leads to a central hall. Windows are spaced equally on either side of the door.

In the second, the 'Side Hall' plan, the front door of the house is located off-centre on the short side of the rectangle, and opens onto a side hall and stairway. The Side Hall houses were usually plainer in appearance than their symmetrical counterparts. These two basic plans were often extended to the rear to become L- or T-shaped houses, designed as such to increase space and improve light and ventilation. Both plans could be dressed up in the style of the day with the addition of ornament, such as decorative bargeboards on the eaves or fretwork on the verandas.

The third house style is the 'Four Square' (photo p. 208). These square (or almost square) houses were usually larger than their rectangular companions, and were topped by a hipped or truncated roof. They often had a south-facing, symmetrically composed façade and central staircase. Most were two or two-and-a-half storeys tall. Sometimes, especially in the towns, they were dressed up with details such as bay windows and roof dormers.

Island houses were usually constructed of a wooden frame sheathed with wood siding. Two basic framing types were common: balloon framing and, after 1890, platform framing. Balloon framing permitted quick and easy construction of the exterior frame and the addition of the roof before interior work was begun. The actual construction procedure entailed the attachment of very long two-by-four studs to a sill plate that was secured to the foundation. The stud walls extended in one piece up to the plate supporting the roof. Floor joists, supported by ribbon boards, were nailed to the individual studs. The newer plat-

The 'Side Hall' house

form framing procedure eliminated the need for long two-by-fours and also permitted construction in stages, floor by floor, since each succeeding storey was framed on the completed storey below.

Houses were occasionally built of stone or veneered with brick or concrete. In many fieldstone houses, rubble of varying size was bonded with large amounts of mortar, which resulted in rough walls that were sometimes covered with plaster outside and lath and plaster inside. Neater, more elegant fieldstone houses required the skills of a mason.

Concrete was popular as a house veneer over the standard wood framing. It was a relatively inexpensive treatment, as lime for the cement was produced locally in lime kilns (firing ovens) from island rock. A kiln was basically a large rock oven with mud-packed sides and a crude grate in which limestone rocks were burned for seven days. Often the cement was dressed up with paint or tooling to give the appearance of stone or brick. Some turn-of-the-century houses were made of cement blocks, moulded like bricks with their exterior face pressed to look like stone.

A cement house was constructed with a regular frame, but forms were wired onto the outside of the framing. A veneer of cement 10 cm (4 inches) thick was then poured into the forms. If the house was to be more than one storey, the forms would be removed after the first-floor veneer was poured and reused for the second (and third) floors, right up to the peak of the gables. Provisions for doors and windows were made by simply building those apertures into the forms. Frames, sashes, and doors were then fitted later by the carpenters. You can often still see the marks in the cement from the wooden plank forms, and even some of the remaining wire ties which held them.

For those interested in early Ontario architecture, I recommend *At Home in Upper Canada*, by Jeanne Minhinnick; *The Ancestral Roof*, by Marion MacRae and Anthony Adamson; *Building with Wood*, by John I. Rempel; *Canada Builds*, by Thomas Ritchie; and *Ontario Architecture: A Guide to Styles and Building Terms*, by John Blumenson.

SIX

The La Cloche Mountains

The northern entrance to Manitoulin
Island, through the La Cloche Mountains
to Little Current

Highway 6, from McKerrow on the Trans-Canada Highway to
Little Current on Manitoulin Island, is often termed Ontario's
most scenic 50 km (31 miles). It runs from the granite and
quartzite Canadian Shield landscape of the North Shore to the
limestone land on Manitoulin, two landscapes adjacent yet
extremely different in terrain and vegetation.

Espanola, with a population of about six thousand, is the largest community in the Manitoulin area. Located between Sault
Ste Marie and Sudbury about 5 km (3 miles) south of the
Trans-Canada Highway, it was established because of the Spanish River's waterfalls, which were harnessed for their power. In
1899 W.J. Sheppard and George R. Gray started what became
the Spanish River Paper Company, building a dam and mill in
1901. The town's history has been tied to the mill ever since.

Until 1912, when the first two paper machines began producing newsprint, the mill was devoted exclusively to wood cutting.
Between 1903 and 1904 a boarding house and thirty-one brick
homes were constructed. The bricks were made of the clay removed for the power canal and sand from a pit in the middle of
the town. The mill was expanded in 1927 when it was purchased
by the Abitibi Power and Paper Company. Increased operating
costs and decreased demand for newsprint forced the mill to
close in 1932.

During the Second World War the vacant mill became a prisoner-of-war camp, housing twelve hundred persons. It was purchased in 1943 by the Kalamazoo Vegetable Parchment Company. The mill is currently operated by E.B. Eddy Forest Products Limited and produces specialty paper products, kraft pulp, and fine papers, including food and medical packaging products and parchment. The mill was modernized and enlarged in 1981. It now contains some of the most sophisticated pollution controls in the world. The company offers tours of its pulp and paper mill, its forest, and the Nairn Centre sawmill. Information is available at the tour office on Tudhope Street.

Espanola was unincorporated until 1958. The northern half of the community was a company town, meaning there was no municipal government, no private property; the mill controlled all utilities, housing, and decisions. The area south of Second Street was an unorganized township. Today, the town provides all the services a tourist could require, including tennis courts, an outdoor pool, and a nine-hole championship golf course. The surrounding area has beaches, hiking on the Rainbow Trail, boating, canoeing on the Spanish and Aux Sauble rivers, fishing, and hunting.

From Espanola on Highway 6 south you will travel over, through, and around the massive granitic La Cloche Mountains, and past countless lakes – Apsey, Anderson, and Loon, to name just a few in Merritt Township. At Raven Lake the highway meanders between Mongowin Township on the west and Curtin Township on the east.

About 8 km (5 miles) south of Espanola you may take a 6 km (3.5 miles) detour east, over Tower Mountain into Willisville. This is the entrance for boaters to the Frood–Cranberry Lake chain. Willisville was also once a company town but is now privately owned. Since 1978 Willisville has hosted the La Cloche Country Art Show for ten days every summer. The theme of the show is the portrayal of the La Cloche area, which includes everything from plants to local legends. The show is now held in the Whitefish Falls Community Centre.

The Whitefish River First Nation (Reserve No. 4) begins at the village of Whitefish Falls. You may wish to stop and admire these falls, which are located directly under the highway bridge and next to a small park. The narrow road over the one-lane bridge in town used to be the main highway. This is a main entry point to the North Channel, through the Bay of Islands. Although the amount of water gives the impression of travel over a series of islands, you are actually on the La Cloche Peninsula until you reach Great La Cloche Island. Most of this peninsula belongs to the Whitefish River First Nation. Just southwest of Whitefish Falls was Wallace Mine, where Ontario's first nickel deposit was found in 1847.

The town of Birch Island (Wawaskinaga) is at the intersection of the highway and two famous water areas, the Bay of Islands to the west and McGregor Bay to the east. This is also the junction of the ancient northern Precambrian shield and the younger Palaeozoic rocks of the La Cloche Peninsula and Manitoulin Island. Observe the dramatic change in landscape; the granite and quartzite ridges of the Canadian Shield are replaced by limestone plains and cliffs. Wawaskinaga has a long history of native settlement. During the early part of this century the most powerful medicine man on the North Shore, Mit-ig-o-mish, lived here. He was renowned for his powers, which included healing and long-distance communication. Where the highway takes a sharp turn left is the Roosevelt Memorial. This monument was erected in honour of U.S. president Franklin Delano Roosevelt, who vacationed in the area in 1943. Nearby is St Gabriel Lalement Church. This pretty stone building was built entirely of local materials in 1940 through the generosity of an American summer resident, a Mr McMannus, and local labour.

To visit Dreamer's Rock, first stop at the Whitefish River First Nation office at Birch Island to ask permission and pay the admission fee. Dreamer's Rock stands at the southern tip of the peninsula, on the east end of Cloche Bluff, and may be reached by following the Birch Island Lodge road and taking the left fork. It is the highest visible peak, a huge granite boulder beside the waters of McGregor Bay. In the past, native youths would climb this rock, dream, and discover their guardian spirit and purpose of life. According to Algonquin legend, Kitche Manitou (the Great Spirit) had a vision of the universe which led to its creation (see Manitou-miniss chapter).

The Swift Current Causeway to Great La Cloche Island takes

Dreamer's Rock

you to a privately owned island wildlife sanctuary, which extends for the next 10 km (6 miles), and comprises more than 10,125 ha (nearly 25,000 acres). At the junction of the mainland and Great La Cloche Island, on Highway 6, a National Historic Site marker indicates the 'Route of the Voyageurs,' the canoe waterway of French fur trappers and traders travelling between Quebec and the West. The smooth, level rock surface of Great La Cloche Island was created by the movement of the glaciers.

Great La Cloche Island has a long history as a native settlement and post of the fur trade. The North West Company built a fur trading fort here around 1790. When the company amalgamated with its competitor, the Hudson's Bay Company, in 1821, the post was moved 14 km (9 miles) northwest onto the mainland to join the existing HBC post there. According to records in the Hudson's Bay Company Archives, Alexander Henry Sr reported in 1761 reaching 'an Indian inhabited island, called La Cloche, because there is here a rock, standing on a plain, which being struck, rings like a bell.'

Alexander Henry (1739–1834), a fur trader, was born in New Jersey but went to Quebec as a merchant to supply the British Army. He was one of the first English traders to trade in the northwest. The 'bell rock' he described was used by the natives to sound alarms, and could be heard from Birch Island to Manitoulin. While Dreamer's Rock was a once-in-a-lifetime experience for native youths, Bell Rock was in common use, although the actual ringing was done by a chief or messenger, either as a warning or to announce a meeting or ceremony. Bell Rock remains on Great La Cloche Island across the channel from Dreamer's Rock, though its present form is believed to have been altered by environmental forces. It was originally a single glacial granite boulder, but has now been split by frost or erosion and no longer 'rings.' Local residents say it was last used in the 1890s.

Great La Cloche Island has challenged many over the years. The British attempted to establish a colony, the island's timber was harvested, and prospectors searched here and the neighbouring North Shore for gold. For a time gold stocks such as Bousquet Mines were a popular Manitoulin commodity and many islanders counted prospecting or investing among their

The Bell Rock was a popular feature of local postcards by the 1920s.

vocations. More recently, a wildlife sanctuary was established. Bison were imported to the sanctuary but have not thrived.

As you leave Great La Cloche Island, the highway crosses Goat Island Channel and takes a sharp left turn onto Goat Island, followed by a sharp right and then across the North Channel bridge to Manitoulin. The bridge's history is described in the Little Current tour. At the turn of the century Goat Island was the site of a large encampment, assembled in conjunction with Little Current's annual 1 July festivities, whose inhabitants were famous for their expertise in racing flat-bottomed, double-ended mackinaw boats.

SEVEN

Little Current

In Little Current, the tourist information building near the bridge is a good first stop to obtain information on accommodation and current events for the entire island. Then it is a good idea to drive downtown and park. Parking on the main thoroughfare is at a premium in the summer, but side streets should be relatively empty. You may wish to walk through downtown and along the harbour. The ambitious tourist can walk for several kilometres to the west, below the churches on Robinson Street, to Spider Bay Marina and the ruins of the former mills west of Spider Bay.

This site was named Wewebjiwang or 'where the waters flow back and forth' by the natives; 'Le Petit Courant' by voyageurs who passed by on their fur-trading routes; 'Dingwall' by the post office (though the name was not sanctioned); 'Shaftesbury' by surveyor T.J. Patten, who laid out the townsite. But since the 1860s the town at the North Channel's narrowest point, where the current slows or reverses, has been known as 'Little Current' by its residents. Little Current was originally settled about 140 years ago by native entrepreneurs taking advantage of its harbour. They were joined by non-native settlers about 15 years later. Little Current, like Manitowaning to the southeast, grew quickly; the former had the main steamer landing, the latter the

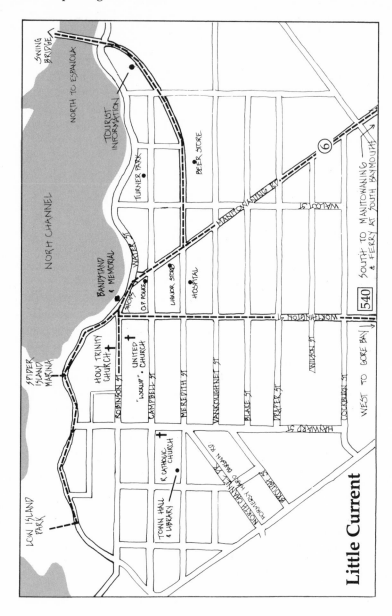

Little Current

land office. Water and trade have always been the town's life: Little Current was a supplier of fuel for steamships, a shipper and miller of lumber, a coal transhipment centre, a water-based tourist destination, and, always, a market town.

Wewebjiwang was established when George Abbotossway, his family, and friends settled here in the early 1850s to supply wood for the steamers which passed through the channel. George was accompanied by his wife and extended family, including grandfather Eddie Ochiltree, who acted as 'chief, medicine man, conjurer and prophet.' They were the first permanent residents recorded on the site of Little Current. Born in Michigan about 1826, Abbotossway was the town's first entrepreneur. He had emigrated to Manitowaning where he received his education from an Anglican missionary. Sarah Newman, his Irish wife, was born in Cobourg, Ontario, and had been employed by the missionary. By 1853 Little Current consisted of George's shanty, six birchbark wigwams, and a clearing.

The Hudson's Bay Company asked for and received permission to build a post in Little Current in 1856. The Post Building, which was a storehouse and factor's residence, was completed and its wharf almost finished two years later. Residents complained, however, that the HBC post would encroach on native trade and land, so the company's licence of occupation was withdrawn before any goods had been moved from nearby Fort La Cloche. From 1860 to 1865 the post was a store and residence, then it was converted into a comfortable family home and occupied for the next seventy years until it burned down in 1942. The site of this former post, behind the *Manitoulin Expositor* office on the main street, bears a plaque to commemorate its history.

The island's second post office opened in Little Current in 1864. It was operated by John Burkitt, the schoolmaster, who was also the first recorded non-native male settler of Little Current. John had been hired as schoolmaster for Manitowaning in 1842. He settled in Little Current in 1862 as the Anglican Church Diocesan Society schoolmaster and catechist.

In January 1865, Jabez Waters Sims, an Anglican missionary, recorded thirteen native families at Little Current: Abotossway, Columbus (Ooshkewahbik), Cooper (Kahgaheway), Eshkemah, Manitowaussen, McGraw, Metahbe, Minegroud, Mukkudabin (Black), Oogemah, Sack (Sacquabunesse), Salter, and Shew-etabgaw; and four non-native families: Burkitt, Dempsey, May, and McKenzie.

Little Current, or Shaftesbury, was first surveyed in 1864–5. The actual town plot consisted of the former Hudson's Bay Company store and wharf, George Abbotossway's stockade and wharf, a powder or ice house, and the fenced lands of George Abbotossway, James Columbus (Ooshkewahbik), Henry Ishke-mah, Joseph Shewetahgun, and John Black (Mocotabin).

By 1868 Little Current contained more than a dozen non-native settlers as well as its original residents, most of whom moved 7 miles west to the new Sucker Creek reserve by 1870. The 1871 census recorded Little Current's population as includ-ing a shoemaker, a butcher, a carpenter, a minister, lumbermen, fishermen, a well digger, labourers, sailors, coopers, teamsters, and an 'Indian Chief.' When William E. Saunders visited in 1880 he described the town as having two nice hotels and quite a number of houses, with a few Indian wigwams about one-half mile to the east.

Little Current in 1886: stores, hotels, wharves, and warehouses stretched along the waterfront.

The town's location on the steamer route guaranteed its importance as a market town, but it was lumber which boosted the economy during the next few decades. According to F.W. Major, author of *Manitoulin, the Isle of the Ottawas*, Little Current's sawmill history began around 1874 when John Amos built a small mill, which was joined a few years later by John Dawson's. In 1886 Charles Anderson of Anten Mills (near Barrie, Ontario) built the town's first big sawmill, the Little Current Planing Mill, known as the Red Mill. Two other large mills were built shortly after. By 1890 these large mills made Little Current an important Lake Huron centre, processing twenty million feet of pine per year. Little Current was dubbed Sawdust Town by its friendly rival Gore Bay, concurrently dubbed Tin Horn Town for its brass band. The ruins of these former mills can be viewed on the western waterfront.

The swing bridge to Little Current has a long history. A charter was granted to the Manitou and Northshore Railway in 1881 to cross the North Channel and connect the island to the mainland. After three decades of setbacks the line finally opened for

The first train crossing the new bridge in 1913 created a permanent link to the mainland after decades of dependence on the shipping season.

passengers and freight as the Algoma Eastern Railway in September 1912. It did not actually reach Little Current until 1913, via the newly constructed railway bridge designed by the firm of Boller, Hodge, and Baird of New York. The trip to Sudbury took four hours. The highway to Espanola from Little Current opened in 1929 with a small car-ferry crossing the North Channel – there was no automobile bridge. In 1945 the bridge was converted to carry both rail and road traffic; it was the fourth of its kind in Canada. At this time its operation was reversed: before 1945 the bridge was left open for boats to pass unless it was needed by a train; after 1945 the bridge remained in position for rail and road traffic and opened on the hour for boats. In 1980 the railway service was discontinued, and the bridge now serves automobile traffic only. In 1983 the swing bridge was designated an Ontario Heritage structure.

Just west of the bridge is the Manitoulin Tourist Information Centre, which opened in 1990. Designed by architect Chris Browne, it features a ceiling 5 metres (16 feet) high centrally supported by a pine pole 1 metre (3 feet) in diameter which was harvested on the Wikwemikong Peninsula.

The land mass opposite the downtown marina is Goat Island, the site of the former coal docks where millions of tons of coal arrived by lake freighters to be transferred to trains for shipment throughout the North Shore of Lake Huron. In 1913 terminal facilities were built by Algoma Eastern Terminals Ltd, a subsidiary of the Algoma Eastern Railway. The 100-foot derrick which was erected had a huge clam-shell-type bucket which could retrieve about three tons of coal per load from the ship's hold and deposit it on the shore. In June 1914 the first ship was unloaded using this facility. Goat Island was also a busy transfer point from which island silica was sent to ports in the United States and paper from the Espanola mill was shipped to customers.

In the early decades of the twentieth century dozens of boats as well as giant log booms would pass through the Channel daily. Occasionally the wind and thus the Channel's current changed direction, halting the flow of logs. Such a disaster could block the Channel for several days. At these times, the appropriateness of Little Current's original name, Wewebji-

In 1914 the Algoma Eastern Railway's Terminal was opened. Coal-bearing lake freighters were unloaded and their cargo transferred to trains for shipment in the North Shore region.

wang, or 'where the waters flow back and forth,' was most apparent.

In July 1906 the federal government responded to numerous complaints about logs blocking the channel by designating Little Current a federal harbour. John T. May was the first harbour master.

Downtown on Water Street, Little Current's main street, two businesses have been in operation since 1879, Turner's store and the *Manitoulin Expositor*. The *Expositor* is also the oldest continuously published newspaper in Northern Ontario. It was established in 1879 in Manitowaning by W.L. Smith, and was purchased in 1888 by Stuart Jenkins, who moved it to Little Current. In 1893 Jenkins sold out to W.A.M. Bellwood, who relocated the plant to the second floor of Miss Potts's store, three doors west of the present United Church. Two years later he increased the paper's extent from four to eight pages.

Turner's store was established by Isaac Turner (1827–1905) and his wife, Elizabeth Hawkins (1830–96). The present store,

Jehiel Tinkis's Mansion House claimed to be the best accommodation in the North Shore area when it opened in 1888.

built in 1913 by Gore Bay contractor George Strain, is the third building on this site, the preceding two having been destroyed by fire early in this century. The structure is said to have been built of one-foot-thick concrete walls to prevent fire.

The Anchor Inn was built as the Mansion House in 1888 by Jehiel Tinkis. The building's contractor was, again, George Strain of Gore Bay. On its opening the Mansion House claimed to be the best accommodation available in the North Shore region. Tinkis was born about 1817 near Ottawa, and was employed as a police detective before emigrating to Providence Bay in 1880 to open a store. He was a member of Little Current's first council in 1890, became mayor for one term in 1896, and was active in town business with his sons Colin and Doug. In May 1901, D.A. Tinkis illuminated the Mansion House with electricity from the Red Mill. In 1912 the hotel had to rebuild after it was seriously damaged by fire. Jehiel's nephew John Hilliard (Hill) Tinkis ran the inn during the 1930s. Hill was a colourful innkeeper: my grandfather recalled Hill wringing his parrot's neck when it laughed at him for falling down the stairs.

In September 1902 the Merchant's Bank of Canada opened its 76th branch in a temporary building owned by George Kingsbury. The island had long needed a bank, but without road or rail transportation the banks were reluctant to send money by horse over the frozen North Channel. The boom in lumber-mill profits eventually convinced them to take the risk. In January 1904 the bank moved into its new home (the site of the present Bank of Montreal) with the manager's residence on the top floor.

The Wharfside laundry and gift shop building survives from the town's turn-of-the-century commercial boom, when it was the home of John G. Sims's Picture Framing, Undertaking and Fishing Tackle. Sims's boldly painted motto, 'Say Nothing,' was on the building for many years.

The waterfront War Memorial was erected through the efforts of the Every Woman's Club, which was formed in 1921 for that specific purpose. The statue was unveiled in 1922 and sits on the site of the town's first lighthouse. The monument was crafted by the Soo Marble and Granite Works. The following year the club replaced the old bandstand with the present cobblestone-based structure.

The post office is the town's most prominent building – a landmark for its size, location, and function. Designed by a federal Department of Public Works staff architect and built in 1949–50, it is typical of many government buildings constructed after the Second World War. The design is based on the International Style, which stressed an honest expression of structure, function, and materials and the elimination of decoration. The two-storey steel frame structure with a red brick veneer and stone trim was built by the C.G. Carrington Construction Company.

The Manitowaning Road hill (at the east end of the main street), once known as the 'Big Hill,' was a proving ground for the first local automobiles. On its original packed mud and sawdust slope, local residents like merchant Oliver Vincent and lawyer Charles Atkinson would enter into friendly competition in trying to drive up its height.

Little Current was incorporated as a town in 1890. The first council was elected on 28 April 1890, with general merchant Thomas Chapman Sims elected mayor over newspaper publisher Stuart Jenkins. The first council also represented the town's mercantile interests: druggist H. Currie; another general merchant, B.H. Turner; hotel owner Jehiel Tinkis; livery stable keeper Humphrey May; tailor P.C. Conlon; and confectioner W.D. Ritchie.

Begin your tour of the residential area on Robinson Street heading west from downtown. The first residence on the north side of the street at the corner is the Turner house. It was built in 1886 by Charles Anderson, owner of the Red Mill. Before it was completed the Andersons sold it to local merchant Isaac Turner and his wife, Elizabeth Hawkins. Isaac was born in 1827 in Saint John, New Brunswick, of United Empire Loyalist ancestry. His family moved to Pickering, Ontario, around 1842, and Isaac and his wife moved to Little Current in 1879. Isaac was a staunch Baptist and Conservative, and very active in municipal affairs. The family business and home have been passed on from Isaac to his son Byron H. (1864–1920), to his grandson Grant, to his great-grandson Barney, who now manages the business with his son.

On the south side of the street is the United Church, the third church on this site. The original Methodist Church was completed in 1882, constructed of locally quarried limestone. In 1907 a fire destroyed it and eight other downtown buildings; the church was left with only its walls intact. Fire struck again in 1929, destroying the interior and part of the west wall. The church was rebuilt and enlarged, as it appears today. The adjacent parsonage, west of the church, was constructed in 1896, with local sawmill owner Anderson as contractor.

Holy Trinity Anglican Church, which was built in 1886, is across the street. Regular Anglican services began in Little Current in 1864 in a log building downtown. The property for this church was acquired in 1867 by the island's resident Anglican clergyman, Rev. Jabez Waters Sims, who was stationed at Sheguiandah but who held regular biweekly services in Little Current, weather permitting. The Gothic Revival–style church was completed in 1886 by John Dawson, a local sawmill owner. The building costs, furnishings, fonts, and holy vessels were donated by R.A. Jones of London, England, and family of the Hon. Robert Jones (c 1792–1874) of Montreal, former member of the Legislative Council of Lower Canada. The first service was held on 9 January 1887, by the Rev. Canon Frederick Frost. A new parish hall and narthex were dedicated on 21 September 1982. The narthex, built under the supervision of Archie Vermeesch, is a credit to local craftsmanship.

Eleven Robinson was built by Frank and Sarah Gray and featured adjoining back and front parlours, a formal dining room, large farm-style kitchen, breakfast room, and cloakroom. A new convenience, the bathroom, was added later. The Potts house (15 Robinson) housed Miss Potts's store on the main floor in 1893 and W.A.M. Bellwood's *Expositor* newspaper plant on the second floor. The Shaftesbury Inn at 19 Robinson Street was built as a home for surveyor T.J. Patten in 1886. In 1997 the inn was restored and opened by the Argmann family. The town's former jail, and later 'Municipal Building,' is hidden in the residential neighbourhood behind the Potts house. This jail is thought to be the original 'lockup' constructed in 1878 by the Law Building Company of Meaford, Ontario, for the Ontario Department of Public Works. Mr Potts was 'keeper of the lockup' for many years.

On the north side of Robinson Street, just before Hayward Street, watch for a unique lawn ornament. Island craftsman Austin Bateman created this scale replica of Strawberry Island lighthouse.

The first Catholic Church, St Vincent de Paul, was built in October 1890. Following a fire in 1917, a new brick church, St Bernard's, was built on the old foundation. A new St Bernard's Church was built in 1996. It features a floating 'sail' ceiling, a dramatic stone wall, the original pews, and stained glass windows. The Catholic cemetery on North Channel Drive was established in the early 1890s. Before that time, Catholics were sometimes buried in Killarney, on the North Shore. Little Current's first hotel keeper, Brian Mackie, who was killed by a neighbour in 1886, was reburied along with his father in the Catholic cemetery in 1898.

Just west of St Bernard's is the Little Current library. In 1893 a group of citizens led by Presbyterian minister Rev. W.E. Wallace organized a Mechanics Institute. The town was canvassed for donations of books and fifty-cent memberships. The institute was acquired by the town in 1896, destroyed by fire in 1910, and replaced in 1932.

The ruins of the former Red Mill now house a shuffleboard court.

The waterfront tour may be done on foot or by car. Heading west from downtown along the waterfront will lead you to Spider Island Marina. Due west of Spider Island are the remnants of Little Current's sawmill history. The ruins on the Little Current shore are those of the former Red Mill, the town's first big sawmill, built in 1886 by Charles Anderson. Anderson died in 1896, aged 54. He was owner and operator of several island mills and owned extensive property. He was also a building contractor whose projects included the Little Current Public School, Honora School, and United Church manse, as well as a tour-boat owner, town councillor, and school trustee. His wife left Little Current in 1898, and the mill was run by their son-in-law Alf Ryley. The Hope Lumber Company later built a new and larger mill on the Red Mill site.

William Potter of Tottenham built another big sawmill in 1886, on Lighthouse Island. Out on the small island are the ruins of the Picnic Island Mill, the town's third large mill, built in 1886 by J. & T. Conlon of Thorold, Ontario. A small village developed around the mill, which employed about sixty men. Picnic Island Mill burned in 1911.

By 1890 Little Current had become a dominant Lake Huron mill town. The mills operated from spring through fall. During the winter the men worked in lumber camps cutting trees on the North Shore, Manitoulin, and the Clapperton, Fitzwilliam, and La Cloche islands. But in 1896 depression hit, supplies dwindled, and only one mill was running. Around 1903 another boom occurred and Little Current boasted the sawmills, two lath mills, two shingle mills, and a sash and door factory. In 1906 and 1907 the Red and Picnic Mills were purchased by separate Michigan interests and re-equipped; these operated until the 1920s.

The Manitoulin Health Centre on Meredith Street was opened 20 September 1945 as St Joseph's Hospital, and operated by the Sisters of St Joseph. It had a capacity of twenty beds and was located in a renovated residence. The building was constructed around 1896 by Thomas C. Sims, the town's first mayor. In 1982 the many-times renovated house was demolished and replaced by the present modern health facility. The Worthington Street hill just west of the hospital, known as 'Shannon's Hill,' was almost as famous as the adjacent 'Big Hill' of Manitowaning Road for its height and ability to defeat early automobiles.

Little Current's biggest annual civic celebration is Haweater Weekend, held on the first weekend in August and sponsored by the Lions Club. It is believed that early pioneers were once saved from starvation by eating the berries off the hawthorn tree. Today the term Haweater signifies someone born on Manitoulin. As you tour the island watch for these small hardy trees, recognizable by their long spike-like thorns and berries which ripen to a deep red colour in August. The Little Current chapter of the Lions International received its charter in 1938, and began the Haweater Weekend in 1967.

For a final glimpse of Little Current visit Turner Park on Campbell Street East for a view of the town and North Channel.

In 1998 Little Current, Howland Township, and the North Channel Islands amalgamated to form the Town of Northeastern Manitoulin and the Islands or NEMI.

EIGHT

The Scenic North Coast
(Tour 1)

Little Current to Mississagi Strait lighthouse, from the island's northeastern
entrance to the western tip

This is the longest tour (134 km or 83 miles), and the most varied. You may wish to give yourself two days, or more if you
really like to meander and savour the sights. There is a half day
of hiking on this route, as well as numerous beaches. If you have
less time, follow only a portion of this tour, perhaps as far as
Gore Bay. Only part of the tour will actually be spent driving;
exploring the pioneer cemeteries, lookouts, historic farmsteads,
native reserves, ghost ports, hiking trails, boardwalks, waterfalls, communities, lighthouses, and fishing stations is best
accomplished on foot. And remember, this is a rural highway:
around every bend is a surprise.

Restaurants are located in Little Current, West Bay, Kagawong, Gore Bay, and Meldrum Bay, and near the Indian Point
Bridge. There are also numerous waterfront picnic spots. Hiking
and walking trails are found at Cup and Saucer Hill, West Bay,
Kagawong, Gore Bay, and the Mississagi Strait lighthouse.

Little Current to Kagawong

Start at the intersection of Water and Worthington streets (the
Toronto-Dominion Bank corner) in downtown Little Current.
Follow Worthington Street south from downtown to Highway

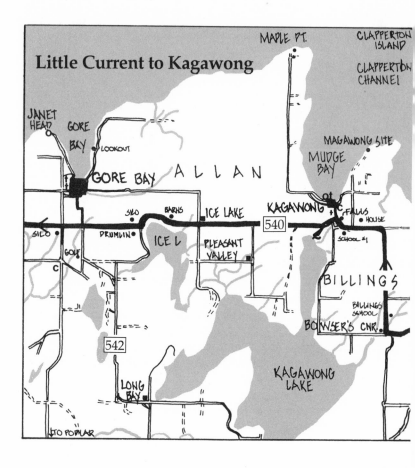

Little Current to Kagawong

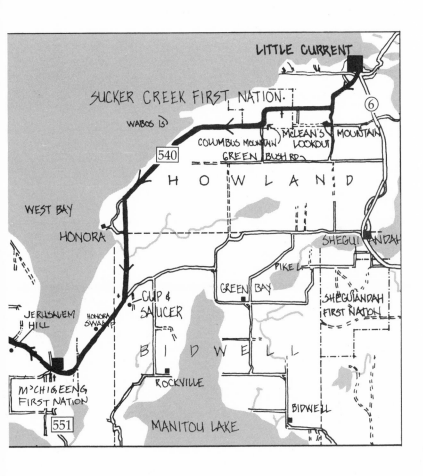

540 west. About 2.2 km (1.3 miles) south of town on the left (east) side of the highway is Holy Trinity Anglican Cemetery, which has been in use since 1868 and for many years was the area's only Christian burial ground. Graveyards can tell a lot about the history of a place and the people who lived there.

This cemetery is the final resting place of many of the town's earliest pioneers, including Donald McKenzie, who was buried here in 1897. Born in 1822 in New Brunswick, he was the first of nine children born to two Scottish immigrants, William and Elizabeth McKenzie. During the 1840s the McKenzie family migrated west via Galt (now Cambridge), Barrie, and Owen Sound. In the 1850s, members of the family decided to go their separate ways. Donald, his wife, Margaret Maria, and their three young children sailed to Manitoulin Island to establish a fish trading station. Manitoulin was a daring venture for the family. The isolated island had been sparsely populated by natives and their religious and government patrons since 1833. The McKenzies settled first at Wikwemikong. Margaret died during the winter while her husband was away trading. She was the first non-native woman buried on the Wikwemikong Peninsula. Donald subsequently married Margaret's sister and moved his family across the bay to Manitowaning. His second wife died one year later in childbirth. Following this tragedy the McKenzie family packed up and moved to Chicago, where Donald had business connections. In December 1864 the family returned to the island, where Donald took up the new position of lighthouse keeper in Little Current. He advertised in the Sault newspaper for a housekeeper, hired, and shortly thereafter married a widow with three young sons. At his death in Little Current at age 75 he had been thrice widowed, raised thirteen children, and witnessed the island's rapid change from isolated native camps to a bustling farming, lumbering, and shipping concern. Take a few minutes to stroll through this neat lot. More recently interred are war veterans, including Lance Corporal Austin Morris Corbiere (1943–66), a casualty of the Vietnam War.

This area belongs to Howland Township, which was surveyed in 1864. It was named for the Hon. Sir William Pierce Howland, who was to become Ontario's lieutenant-governor from 1868 to 1873. Howland Township's first non-native settlers were the May family, headed by Philip and Amelia. They had emigrated to Manitowaning from Penetanguishene, Ontario, in May 1842 to instruct the natives in the cooper or barrel-making trade. In the late 1840s the family left Manitoulin, returning in 1860 to settle in Howland. Descendants of Philip and Amelia May can claim the longest non-native residency on Manitoulin, over 130 years.

McLean's Mountain lookout is the next stop. Continue along Highway 540 for 0.9 km (one-half mile). Where the main highway takes a sharp turn right continue up the hill, straight ahead. Follow the rural road up McLean's Mountain to the lookout. As far back as 1879 the local newspaper proclaimed this view one of the prettiest on the island. From this point, 328 m (1,075 feet) above sea level, you can see West Bay, Little Current, the North Channel, and the islands beyond. This lookout site was donated by John C. and Margorie VanEsterik, and features a picnic area, toilet facilities, and a great view. The area is named for Irish pioneer Samuel McLean (1820–94). Samuel, born in Turlough, Ireland, emigrated to Canada in 1846 (probably to escape the Irish potato famine) and settled here in 1866 with his wife, Mary, and their five children. The McLean farm was located near the base of the mountain, on the east side of the mountain road. A community activist, Sam was a school-board trustee and secretary, Howland municipality treasurer, and Presbyterian Church trustee. He was also active in Little Current's first Sunday School, a unique cooperative project involving three pioneers of different religious affiliations. Rev. Jabez Sims, minister of Sheguiandah's Anglican Church, provided the teaching materials; McLean, a Presbyterian, was the superintendent; and William Rowe, a Wesleyan Methodist, was his assistant.

For an interesting side trip, continue past McLean's lookout and take the second left turn. This will take you east through the Green Bush area to Highway 6, depositing you 5 km (3 miles) south of Little Current. The route takes you through farmlands on the plateau which tops the mountain and ends with a magnificent view of Manitoulin's east coast and the North Channel.

As you descend McLean's Mountain you can see the northeast coast, including Strawberry Island and the channel. Turn left onto Highway 540 heading west. On your immediate left the United Church cemetery provides another spectacular view of the North Channel. The oldest headstone marks the grave of John McLean, son of Samuel, who died in 1880 at the age of 23. Buried here are many early settlers. James Stringer's story provides a glimpse of pioneer life – and death – on the Ontario frontier. James was born in Canada three months after his family emigrated from Armagh, Ireland, in 1849. The family of four fled the Irish potato famine, enduring an arduous thirteen-week voyage aboard the ship *Dublin Weave*, which sank on the return crossing. After landing in Quebec, the Stringers headed west to Brampton, Ontario, where relatives had settled in 1828. In 1856 they purchased a 100-acre lot near Orangeville, Ontario. Two years later the senior Stringer, Robert, died, leaving his widow to raise their five children. The eldest son, John, aged 13, took charge of the family and farm. They had planned to grow wheat but found the land was unsuitable for that and so planted pota-

McLean's Mountain lookout

toes. John was soon known as the 'Potato King of Garry,' an ironic title considering it was the Irish potato famine which had driven his family to Canada.

His brother James and brother-in-law Francis Atkinson headed for Manitoulin in the late 1860s to cut timber. James's promising reports prompted his mother, siblings, and numerous cousins to join him on Manitoulin. In 1875 James married Elizabeth, the daughter of William McKenzie (buried in the Anglican cemetery up the road), and farmed at various island locations before settling directly across the road from this cemetery. James's youngest daughter, Millie, recalled, in later years, that during the first decade of the 1900s her principal chore before school every morning was to help drive the cows from this farm up to pasture on the top of McLean's Mountain.

Highway 540, to the west, follows the base of the Niagara Escarpment, the edge of which is marked by sharp northern coastal cliffs. Between Little Current and Honora this highway runs along and across post-glacial beaches which were created by the receding levels of the glacial lakes that preceded Lake Huron. In traversing the escarpment this rolling highway passes old farms and new country homes. Watch for the island's traditional fences. These cedar rail fences, known locally as snake fences, have been constructed since the earliest pioneers arrived. They are not only picturesque, but also portable and practical. The island has an abundance of cedar for their construction and they can be erected quickly by farmers. There are several variations of construction: no vertical support posts, leaning supports, and upright supports.

About 5 km (3 miles) from Little Current you enter Sucker Creek First Nation (Reserve No. 23), established in 1866 when natives of the Anglican faith in Little Current selected their land according to the terms of an 1862 treaty. Eleven of the twelve families recorded here in the 1871 census had moved from Little Current in the previous three years. A schoolteacher was provided by the Congregational Society of Owen Sound and regular Anglican church services were held by the missionary from Sheguiandah. Sucker Creek consists of 663 ha (1,638 acres) and has a population of about two hundred. On your immediate left is the community's cemetery (ngokaan), marked by pretty white wooden crosses. Across the highway, about 50 metres farther west, lies the overgrown foundation of Sucker Creek's first church. Just ahead on the left is St Luke's Anglican Church. It was built in the 1880s as a school, and was converted to a church in 1953 after a new school was built. Regular Anglican services have been held in Sucker Creek since about 1870. Up on the ridge behind the church is the site of the first community in this area, consisting of a row of whitewashed log cabins. As late as the 1950s many natives resided in log cabins which received an annual spring coat of whitewash. Charles Abbotossway (c 1859–1950), son of George Abbotossway, Little Current's first native entrepreneur, was chief of the Sucker Creek reserve for forty-five years. Charles received notoriety early this century when he visited New York to star in a production of 'Hiawatha' as a publicity stunt for a Canadian railway company. From 1916 to 1921 the Anglican rector, Rev. Canon Eric Montizambert, who was stationed at Little Current and was also rector of Sucker Creek, McGregor Bay, and Whitefish, would walk here from Little Current to conduct services in Ojibwe. His salary of $650 per year was augmented by raising chickens and cultivating a large garden.

This band is currently undergoing a process of revival and unification. The Sucker Creek First Nation of Ojibwes has established Sucker Creek Day, held on the first Friday in June since 1987. In June 1990 Sucker Creek held its first annual powwow and tribal gathering. The community's Waubano Fish Farm has raised and sold rainbow trout since 1992.

The highway takes a sharp left turn at this point. You may, however, want to take a short 1.5 km (1 mile) detour to the right (or north) to enjoy a magnificent view of the channel from Turner Cove. A beautiful shoreside camping and picnic park is located here.

Continuing along the highway you ascend Columbus Mountain. If you visit Manitoulin in the second half of May you may catch one of the island's large trillium beds in bloom. This mountain was named for James Columbus (Ooshkewahbik), who moved from the United States to Manitoulin in the late 1840s with his wife and daughter. The family settled on the island's east coast, and moved to Little Current in the 1850s. Following the 1862 treaty, the Little Current natives selected Sucker Creek as their reserve and James, who was by then Second Chief, moved here. He drowned in 1870, leaving his widow to raise their six children.

Leaving Sucker Creek the road passes the Rowe settlement, a small farming community containing several picturesque tin-sided farmhouses overlooking the North Channel. This community was founded in October 1878 when the English families of Arthur and Julia Rowe and Thomas and Ellen Rowe purchased lots here. Soon William and Matilda Rowe joined the settlement. Besides numerous frame and log outbuildings, there is an old stone root cellar in front of the gold-coloured tin-sided farmhouse.

Directly ahead is another view of the North Channel. As the road bends southwest you glimpse Wabos (Rabbit) Island. Then follow the shore of West Bay for about 6 km (3.5 miles). On a clear day you may see Clapperton Island to the northwest and the opposite shore of West Bay directly to the west. On the left is Manitoulin Honey, where the Bingaman family processes island honey for sale. Honey has been produced commercially on Manitoulin since 1886, when J.A. Cameron of Manitowaning, Robert Rivett of Billings, Ralph Mutchmor of Providence Bay, and Messrs Hall and Willett of Gordon were all practising apiarists. Next, also on the left, is the Manitoulin Ski Club for both downhill and cross-country skiers. The facilities include a T-bar lift, two downhill runs, several kilometres of ski trails, and a beginners' hill.

About 10 km (6 miles) past Sucker Creek is Honora Bay, on West Bay. In the 1890s Honora Bay, a bustling port for trade in fish, forest, and farm products, was considered to be a booming metropolis by locals. This success stemmed from the Herriman wharf and saw and grist mills. The first postmaster, William Graham, was appointed in 1893. The once-thriving port is now principally a summer cottage community with horseback riding available. From the Honora hill the unusual outline of Cup and Saucer Hill is visible. Roadside patches of light purple chicory are predominant here. As you descend Honora hill, the white frame cottage on the left was the locally renowned Birch Grove restaurant, operated by the Hore family in the 1960s. Stands of birch trees ('wiigwaas,' in Ojibwe) are common in this area, and were useful to the natives in earlier times. About 1 km (0.6 miles) farther, where the highway crosses Perch Creek, is the former site of a native sugarbush, recorded by surveyors during the 1864 survey.

Past Honora is Bidwell Township, established in 1864 and named for the Hon. Marshall Spring Bidwell, lawyer, politician, and former Speaker of the House of Commons. The township's first pioneer was John Dunlop, who arrived here alone in 1866 from Seaforth, Ontario. He settled about 10 km (6 miles) east, near Pike Lake. He purchased several lots and was Bidwell's only landowner until 1868, when John Atkinson joined him. Dunlop married Mary May, daughter of Howland Township settler Philip May, in 1868. Descendants of these pioneers still reside on the island.

The panoramic vistas from the Cup and Saucer Hill Hiking Trail are not to be missed. This popular trail, which has been in existence since 1962, is located where Highway 540 meets the Bidwell Road, about 3 km (2 miles) south of Honora. Turn left onto the Bidwell Road and right just a third of a kilometre later, into the parking area. The hill, which is the island's highest lookout, is named for its little hill, or cup, sitting on the big hill, or saucer, below. After the last glacial retreat all of Manitoulin, except for the top of this area, was under Lake Algonquin, whose shoreline would have been about 290 m (950 feet) above current sea level. This is the most outstanding example of the Niagara Escarpment on the island. A 5.5 km (3.3 miles) trail leads to the top, at 351 m (1,150 feet). Retrace your steps or follow the trail as it winds through woods for a further 6.5 km (4 miles). Allow about 3 hours. Certain portions of the trail are quite challenging, and children should be closely supervised; it is not recommended for children under seven years of age. Most of the trail is a gradual uphill walk, but two cliffs must be climbed near the top for the uppermost view. The top viewpoint ends at an unguarded clifftop edge. The main lookout rewards the hiker with a panoramic view south over the Green Bay settlement and Lake Manitou. Be sure to follow the clifftop trail to the west lookouts, where there are exceptional views west over West Bay, Mudge Bay, and beyond. There is an optional 'Adven-

ture Trail' near the summit, where you can squeeze through a
rock chimney or crawl along a narrow ledge. As you descend
from the uppermost cliff follow the westerly sloping trail, which
follows the bluff back to the parking lot while providing breathtaking views of the edge of the highest peak.

Across the highway and just west of Cup and Saucer Hill is
Cold Springs Church and cemetery. The quaint log church was
built as St Andrew's Presbyterian in 1887 on land donated by
the Moore family. Samuel McLean, of McLean's Mountain, a
staunch Presbyterian, drove the Little Current minister here by
horse and cart over a narrow rugged trail to conduct services.
The cemetery's oldest headstone, dating from 1882, belongs to
William J. Sterling, aged 34. An annual religious service and picnic open to all is held in July.

After passing Cold Springs the road leads to the township of

The Niagara Escarpment as seen at Cup and Saucer Hill
is breathtaking.

St Andrew's log church has served the community for over 100 years.

Billings, which extends to the other side of Kagawong. Billings was surveyed in 1864 and named for Elkanah Billings, a lawyer, surveyor, and palaeontologist who interpreted fossils for the Geological Survey of Canada. The Geological Survey was founded in 1842 as a scientific agency to aid in the development of the mineral industry. Billings Township – like most of Manitoulin Island – is liberally strewn with fossils.

This area is also known as the Honora Swamp. Years ago, it was necessary to build special roads to traverse the many areas of swampland on Manitoulin. In 1895, Harold N. Burden described this process in his book *Manitoulin, or, Five years of church work among Ojibway Indians and lumberman, resident upon that island or in its vicinity:* 'corduroy' roads were constructed by first forming a foundation of tree limbs and tops. Several layers of tree trunks were then placed parallel to the direction of the road on this foundation. Finally, more trunks were rolled along the first layer of trunks and placed perpendicular to the road. This formed a flexible and durable road over swamplands.

A caution for cyclists: the east side of the M'Chigeeng (West Bay) hill is 900 m (3000 feet) long with a 5 to 8 per cent grade.

For cyclists continuing west, there are four hills with an 8 per cent grade between M'Chigeeng (West Bay) and Kagawong.

Continue west for about 5 km (3 miles) to M'Chigeeng (silent m), formerly West Bay First Nation (Reserve No. 22), the island's second-largest native settlement. In the fall of 1847 one of Wikwemikong's chiefs, Taibossegai, accompanied by thirty-one natives, moved from Wikwemikong to 'Mechecowetch-enong' or 'hill of the fish harpoon.' The Indian Department's local superintendent had hoped to contain all Roman Catholic natives on the Wikwemikong Peninsula. Taibossegai cited sugar-bush depletion and insufficient quantities of hay for cattle at Wikwemikong as reasons for leaving, while claiming that Mechecowetchenong was rich in both soil and fish. He was correct and his settlement prospered. In January 1870 another superintendent described 'Mitchikewedinong' as a Roman Catholic settlement for industrious natives. The village had a church and the inhabitants were requesting a school. Two weeks later, funds were allocated for a school and teacher. The population of 295 included 32 people who actually resided at 'Obege-wong' and 28 who lived at Mindemoya Lake. Both groups were reported to be considering moving to M'Chigeeng. By the turn of the century the population had risen to 322 and the community was an important Christian centre. The reserve now encompasses 3,400 ha (8,404 acres) with about 1,000 band members.

The village of M'Chigeeng is an island treasure at the junction of Highways 540 and 551. It is the home of the extraordinary Ojibwe Cultural Foundation and several creative galleries and handicraft shops. Kasheese Studio features paintings by artists-in-residence Shirley Cheechoo and Blake Debassige, both internationally renowned artists, as well as numerous other native artists who work in paint, bone, quill, and beading. Blair Debassige's Nimkee Art Gallery and the West Bay Lodge Gift Shop are also worth visiting.

On the east side of Highway 551 is the twelve-sided tipi-shaped Immaculate Conception Church, the parish church of the native Catholic community of M'Chigeeng. Opened in 1972 to replace one destroyed in an explosion the previous year, this church recaptures the ancient native tradition of 'meeting fire-pits,' where people gathered to talk, listen, and learn about the

The tipi-shaped Immaculate Conception Church serves the native Catholic community of M'Chigeeng.

Great Spirit, Kitche Manitou. A visit to this unique church set among the trees, next to the old cemetery, can only be described as a spiritual experience. Note the bell and the statue of the Virgin Mary at the entrance, both relics from the original building. The church was designed by architect Manfred May of North Bay and Father Michael Murray, SJ. A brochure, available at the entrance for a small donation, describes the symbolic meanings of the church and its appointments. The magnificent front doors were carved by Mervin Debassige. The exterior carvings feature the sun, representing the Great Spirit Kitche Manitou as well as Christ. The four powerful rays represent the cardinal points and the cross. The interior carvings are totems of the Anishnaabeg (native people). The top-lit tipi-shaped building allows the community to gather around a central altar. The circular image is everywhere, representing the Creator and the circle of life. The

natural wood interior, two-thirds of which is below ground, signifies the closeness of the Anishnaabeg to mother earth. Broad
steps/seats descend to the central altar. High overhead is the
Thunderbird, the messenger of the Great Spirit Kitche Manitou.
The baptismal font rests on the back of a sculpted wooden turtle, a reminder of the legend of Creation whereby the Anishnaabeg were re-established following the great flood by a spirit
woman settling on the back of a turtle. The walls feature the Stations of the Cross, with the events of Good Friday painted by a
local artist, Leland Bell. Behind the church is a cluster of headstones from the old cemetery, the oldest belonging to George
Corbiere, son of Henry and Mary, who died in 1873 at the age of
19. Henry Corbiere was born around 1824 in Ontario and supported his large family as a trader.

The Ojibwe Cultural Foundation is also located on Highway
551. Since 1974, this organization has provided cultural and
educational resources for the Ojibwe, Odawa, and Potawatamie
people. Visitors are encouraged to tour the gallery and museum
as well as participate in workshops and demonstrations that cel-
ebrate Anishnaabe life. The new building opened in 1999 after
years of community fundraising spearheaded by Mary Lou Fox
and James Debassige. The building's circular plan reflects the
Ojibwe sacred turtle, the four directions, and the circle of life.

Southeast of the Cultural Foundation the M'Chigeeng Hiking
Trails feature main and alternative trails covering about 8 km
(5 miles) through cedar and hardwood forest. The main trail
leads to the top of the bluff, while the alternative leisure trail
features more horizontal landmarks such as an underground
spring with cold water safe to drink. To follow the entire trail,
which leads to the giant 'M'Chigeeng' sign visible on top of the
escarpment from the village, allow about two-and-a-half hours.
Most of the main trail is through a rolling forested landscape,
marked with several signposts which relate native stories. At
the base of a cliff, hikers have the option of climbing rapidly or
following the alternative leisure trail. The ascent should be
attempted only by avid adult hikers and closely supervised
school-age and older children. The rewarding finish to a challenging climb is a panoramic view over West Bay and beyond to
the North Shore.

The M'Chigeeng powwow is a celebration of youth.

South of the trail are the community cemetery and a large residential area. At Cross Hill, a large wooden cross is a vision marker of native spiritual experiences.

Since 1988 M'Chigeeng has hosted a powwow in celebration of youth, on the long weekend in July or September. This family event is a festive rather than a competitive powwow, and has a friendly, vibrant atmosphere for spectators and dancers alike. The powwow commences with a grand-entry procession from the east, signifying the beginning of life. It is led by those who have earned this right, typically veterans or the owner of an eagle staff, an ancient emblem of courage. Listen to the drum. The rhythmic pounding of many sticks on a single drum, accompanied by voices in unison, is not background but the heartbeat of the powwow. Watch for the pair of lead dancers who participate in all the dances. Since 1988, M'Chigeeng's powwow has been held at the base of M'Chigeeng bluff – a spiritual place in Ojibwe legend.

From M'Chigeeng the tour continues west on Highway 540 through the limestone rock cuts. The top of Jerusalem Hill provides an unexpected view of Saugigansing Lake through the mixed forest. In descending the hill you will have a wonderful view of the westerly farmland and the Kagawong Lakeshore Road while the landscape changes from bush to farm or grazing land. Take a sharp right turn north at Bowser's Corner. Thomas Bowser, his wife, Sarah Hutchinson, and their son John moved here in 1877 from King Township, Ontario, following dozens of others who had emigrated to Kagawong from King Township to work in the local mill and to homestead neighbouring farms.

After the turn the road crosses Mud Creek. On the right is the former Billings School No. 2, constructed in 1900 by William Baillie Sr for $528. It replaced an earlier school located farther north in a field. In 1949 the school was closed and its students bussed to Kagawong. Originally faced with cedar shingles, most of the building has been reclad. On the south side of the former school a stone memorial topped by a bell marks the site of the Billings Church, which served residents from 1912 to 1971. The fields of stumps are visible reminders of the pioneer hardship of land clearing.

The highway takes a sharp left, taking you from flat bushland to gently rolling farmland. Watch for shingle-sided and -roofed buildings. Shingles were an extremely popular siding material for houses on Manitoulin. The island's earliest industries were saw and shingle mills, and the cedar shingles produced in these mills had an excellent reputation for durability. The slow growth of cedar on Manitoulin produced a denser and therefore longer-lasting product than the quick-growing species found on Canada's west coast. Manitoulin's remaining shingle-sided buildings stand as a testament to this early industry.

Approaching Kagawong, the road takes another sharp turn north where, on the left, is Billings School No. 1. This stone school was built in 1902 to replace the original 1877 school building, which was located down the hill from this site. In 1924 the building was damaged by fire and repaired. A new two-room addition was built in 1963, but the school was closed in 1969.

A short half-kilometre from this corner, on the right side, is another island highlight, Bridal Veil Falls. A small park is located here, with picnic grounds and toilet facilities. Stairs lead down to the base of the falls where visitors can walk behind the cascading waters. Bridal Veil Falls, 20 m (65 feet) high, is on the Kagawong River, which runs 3 km (2 miles) from Lake Kagawong to Mudge Bay on the north shore of the island. Lake Kagawong is the island's second largest lake, but its river drainage, unlike that of lakes Manitou and Mindemoya, is forced northward. Its course through the limestone edge of the escarpment produces these powerful falls. A hiking trail along the river leads into town past a small private generating station which sells its electricity to Ontario Hydro. This scenic, well-travelled route takes about 30 minutes to follow. Alternatively, one can drive into 'Kag' by following the road straight north (although the main highway to Gore Bay bends left after the falls). The falls gave rise to the village of Kagawong, first by powering mills and later providing electric power for the island. The picnic area is on the site of Kagawong's lumber and grist mill, built by the Henry brothers in 1873.

William and Robert Henry, two sawmill owners from King Township near Toronto, were granted 800 acres of land in the adjacent townships and a mill seat in Kagawong, provided they also built a grist mill and brought in twelve settlers. They built their mill on top of the west bank of Bridal Veil Falls. By November 1874 the sawmill was operating, as were the gristing facilities by 1875. Settlers soon arrived to work in their lumbering industry and establish farms.

Both Henry brothers died tragically in shipwrecks: one drowned on the *Manitoulin* in May 1882 and the other on the *Asia* in September 1882. In fact, the entire history of the Henry family in Canada was a saga of tragedy. The family of eight left Armagh, Ireland, in 1847 to escape the potato famine. By the time the family settled in Ontario, both parents and two children had been lost to the perils of immigration. The surviving

Bridal Veil Falls

four boys eventually settled into farming and lumbering near Toronto. They relocated on Manitoulin after a fire destroyed their mill in Vaughan. Robert Henry died a bachelor, and William left a widow and five children living in southern Ontario. William's son, George Henry (1871–1953), served in the provincial legislature for thirty years, from 1913 to 1943, and was the premier of Ontario from 1930 to 1934. He provided the province with its first highway system and Canada's first concrete bridge. He is best remembered, however, as Ontario's Depression-era premier.

Following the deaths of William and Robert Henry, William's wife, Louisa, owned the mill until 1896, when she sold it to James Carter. Carter, who was born in 1858 in Elgin County, Ontario, had previously operated mills on Tobacco and Wolsey lakes. His large wood-frame residence, built in 1899, stands on the northwest corner of the highway intersection. The Carter family was known for the many civic improvements they undertook in Kagawong.

Kagawong

Kagawong has retained its beautiful Ojibwe name, which translates as 'where mists rise from the falling water.' Long before the Henry brothers established their mill, Kagawong was a native village, one of three on Mudge Bay. When this township was surveyed in 1867 Kagawong was a native village of four houses and three families who, at the time, were considering relocating to West Bay. They had large gardens of potatoes and corn about 2 km (1.2 miles) south on the east shore of Lake Kagawong and a sugarbush west of the village. The area's first non-native settler was a French Canadian, Luke Chatreau, who built a cabin about 1872 to the southwest on Lake Kagawong. He had first settled in Howland Township in 1866 with his wife, Margaret, and their children. They operated a sailboat which transported settlers west from the Little Current steamer landing. In June 1880 the *Manitoulin Expositor* noted that 'Luke Chartraun, the first settler on Lake Kagawong, had been buried at West Bay.'

The circle route along Lower Main Street and Upper Street is an interesting way to see the town. Downtown's Lower Main

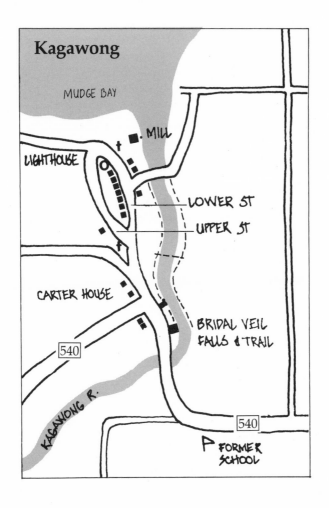

Street presents a well-preserved view of turn-of-the-century commercial architecture, while Upper Street features a scenic residential area overlooking Mudge Bay. Mudge Bay was named for a British admiral by Captain Henry Bayfield during a charting expedition in 1817–22. The town plot of Kagawong was laid out in 1879 by public land surveyor George Brockett Abrey. The settlement quickly prospered in lumbering, shipping, and tourism. An 1884–5 directory described Kagawong, or Mudge Bay, as a village of 250 persons with a church, school, saw-mill, and two general stores. In 1892 most of the lower part of town was destroyed by a fire, but within four years most of the present buildings had been constructed. The community museum, located in the former Spring Bay post office, features exhibits on postal transportation and local history.

The first building on the west side of Lower Main Street has at various times housed a photography shop, a leather and harness shop, and a residence. The neighbouring wood-frame building with double veranda was built as a store around 1896 and functioned as such until 1952. It was constructed for the Miller family, merchants in Gore Bay, and was run initially by Jesse Lehman. Lehman, who arrived on Manitoulin in 1877 with his family, later operated a blacksmith shop, which still stands across the street. In the age of the automobile the blacksmith shop became Art Elliott's garage, which existed until about 1959.

The Bridal Veil Antique Store was built as a general store and post office by William Boyd following the 1892 fire. The first Kagawong post office had been opened in 1876 by James McInnes. In September 1891 William Boyd was appointed post-master, a position which remained in his family for 81 years. After William's death in 1925, his wife, Annie, became postmistress until 1953, and was succeeded by his daughter Vera until her retirement in 1972.

Park's Folly Bed and Breakfast, a gabled building with verandas, was built around 1910 for Thomas Thompson. The stone Needle's Rathskellar block was built about 1925 by Hugh Brown as a butcher shop. It has served many purposes, including poolroom, ice-cream parlour, and grocery store.

The former Havelock Hotel, a large frame three-storey gabled building originally owned by John Hilliard, stands next door. Hilliard purchased a small hotel in Kagawong in 1887, which he operated until the 1892 fire destroyed it and most of the village. In 1896 he built the Havelock Hotel, which his son William continued to operate after John's death in 1911. Hilliard's Havelock had a wide reputation as one of the best tourist resorts on the continent for fishermen seeking smallmouth bass. The hotel is built of local materials, including stone and lumber. The first floor has a bar, store, office, and parlour. The second floor has fifteen rooms and two common bathrooms.

The wood-frame building on the shore side of the street, across from the stone block, was the livery stable for the Havelock Hotel. The agricultural hall is located between the livery stable and the church.

St John the Evangelist Church has a nautical theme: its pulpit is the bow of a boat, and its pews are decorated with fishing buoys.

Hunt's Store and post office building, the former Snow Store built after the 1892 fire by Charlie and Hattie (Harriet Thompson) Snow, is now operated by township reeve Austin Hunt. The wife of the Havelock Hotel owner was the sister of Charlie Snow, and Charlie himself was a Havelock Hotel tenant before his marriage.

The Anglican Church of St John the Evangelist, which opened in 1938, was originally a warehouse for Charlie and Harriet Snow's store located across the street. The one-and-a-half storey frame warehouse was built around 1898 and was later sold for one dollar to the church committee. It received hardwood flooring, wallboard, a stove, and a belfry: the church bell came from a railroad locomotive. In the 1950s and 1960s a nautical theme was adopted. The ship's wheel over the door was salvaged from a pulp barge that sank in the bay outside the church; the pulpit is the bow of a boat wrecked near Maple Point in 1965; and the buoys on the pews came from the local Graham Brothers' fishing nets. The red neon cross was purchased with insurance money to replace the original wooden cross which was struck by lightning.

Beside the harbour is the former Manitoulin Pulp Company mill. In 1923 James Carter, owner of the mill site at the falls, offered his water power free to any company that would establish a new industry in Kagawong. The offer was accepted by the Little Rapids Pulp Company of Wisconsin, which built a pulp mill on the site in 1925. Constructed of local limestone in less than one year, it ran on water power from the original Henry mill. The pulp was shipped to Green Bay, Wisconsin, for use in Sears-Roebuck catalogues. The mill went bankrupt in 1930, and the building was bought by Ontario Hydro in 1946 and used as a generating station until 1961. Until 1951 the installation supplied the island with its electricity. The building was renovated in 1991 to serve as a community centre. On the shore beside the mill are a picnic area, playground, and public beach.

The Kagawong cemetery is located east of the mill. Some of the area's first settlers are buried here, including Robert Rivett (1824–1910), his wife, Ann, and their family. Robert arrived in 1875 from King Township in southern Ontario, one of the twelve settlers required of the Henry brothers in their milling contract.

At the end of Lower Main Street is the Kagawong lighttower. First lit on 29 October 1894, it replaced the previous light, which had been erected in 1888 on the same site but which had been destroyed in the fire of 1892. Kagawong's original lighttower was built in June 1880 on the Kagawong dock. The present structure was constructed by the federal Department of Marine and Fisheries at a cost of $293.81. The square pyramidal wood building is topped by a wood lantern whose light was designed to be visible for almost 18 km (11 miles).

'Kag' has always been a lumbering and shipping port. It was also well known for Berry boats, which were made here by Oliver Berry (1877–1957). Oliver and his family lived and worked on the flats near the present pulp mill site. They produced fishing and pleasure boats 18 to 25 feet long of high quality cedar and white oak. The construction of the pulp mill forced the Berrys to move their house and shop up the hill, a task which required almost three dozen horses and two days of labour. The family boat business was later taken over by Oliver Berry Jr, and is still in operation.

A walk along Upper Street gives a view of Mudge Bay and many houses that are nearly one hundred years old. Near the end of the street is a beautiful residence with a white two-sided veranda, built of island limestone for Jack Allen.

North of Kagawong, past the waterfront, is the former native camp-site of Maple Point (Maimonakeking). This village had thirty-eight residents in 1846, and seventy-two by the 1860s when the band moved to West Bay (now M'Chigeeng). Today Maple Point is home to numerous summer and permanent residents. In the 1930s Maple Point was the summer home of Daniel (Danny) George Dodge (1917–38), son of John Francis Dodge of Dodge automobile fame – and the setting for one of the island's greatest tragedies. Danny, an heir to the Dodge fortune, enjoyed tinkering with motor boats, automobiles, and airplanes, and loved Manitoulin for its unspoiled, remote beauty. In 1935 Danny bought a hunting lodge and acreage at Maple Point, and three years later married a Gore Bay resident, Laurine MacDonald. On his honeymoon at the lodge Danny was critically wounded in a dynamite accident. He was loaded into his high-powered motor boat with his new bride at the wheel, and the two set off for a fast run to Little Current in search of a doctor. Danny, delirious with pain, fell overboard and drowned en route.

Another former native camp-site, the Magawong camp, is located northeast of Kagawong on the point dividing Mudge Bay and West Bay. Mudge Bay and Lake Kagawong have always been popular with fishermen in search of yellow perch, pickerel, smallmouth bass, splake, northern pike, and, in the spring, smelts.

Farther uphill, overlooking the bay, is the settlement's first church, St Paul on the Hill, which opened in 1884. The site and wood were donated by the Henry brothers on condition that the church be made available to all denominations, although it was deeded to the Methodists. The Anglicans held morning service and the Methodists afternoon service here for many years. James Johnston was the head carpenter as well as the builder of the pews.

Kagawong has several nearby lookouts worth visiting. Travel northwest from the lighthouse corner along the bay road. Follow the road inland and up two steep hills towards Maple Point. At the top of the second hill on your right (east) is a great view over Mudge and Honora bays. Three km further on your left (west) is a second lookout also worth visiting.

Leaving Kagawong, note the buildings at the intersection of Highway 540. On the east corner stands a small cement building which was Mr Rumbo's Harness and Shoe repair shop; on the west, a large wood-frame store, the Billings Company Store, built by the second mill owner, James Carter, around 1896; and on the northwest corner, a large shingle-clad home, the former residence of James Carter. Just west of the corner is the present home of Berry Boats. Across from Bridal Veil Falls is the boat launch for the Kagawong River, which leads to Kagawong Lake. In 1993, the Ministry of Natural Resources declared four island rivers to be fish sanctuaries: the Kagawong River, the Manitou River, sections of the Mindemoya River, and Blue Jay Creek. The period between September 25 and October 31 was set aside to protect the chinook salmon during spawning.

Kagawong to Gore Bay

After visiting Kagawong, turn west onto Highway 540 again. After 1.5 km (1 mile) the road enters Allan Township, established in 1867 and named for the Hon. George William Allan, a senator from Toronto. The road crosses limestone and bush plains where, for 6 km (3.5 miles), a second growth of forest lines the road. Before it was settled, the island was covered with a large variety of coniferous and deciduous trees including sugar maple, beech, red oak, yellow birch, pine, hemlock, and white spruce in the uplands. Dry areas featured jackpine, and the swamps contained white cedar, elm, white and black ash, and red maple. Today there are two types of second growth: large areas of softwood such as cedar, white spruce, balsam, fir, trembling aspen, poplar, and birch, and hardwood forests of maple and beech. Near the Pleasant Valley Road junction surveyors' records reported a large native sugarbush in 1867. On the south side of the highway between Mike's Park Road and the Pleasant Valley Road, a mysterious fire can often be seen burning in the evening. This swamp gas fire is a natural gas spring that is periodically ignited and results in numerous fire alarms reported by unsuspecting drivers. You can often spot deer on the Pleasant Valley Road at dusk.

The small farming community of Ice Lake, located about 8 km (5 miles) west of Kagawong, is named for its small shallow lake whose water is the first to freeze in the fall and thaw in the spring. The earliest settlers were Tom Wilson, John Dearing, and John Nelson. In 1874 John Nelson married Lizzie Wilson, and three years later homesteaded in Ice Lake, building a log shanty with a trough roof. A trough or scoop roof consisted of logs split in half lengthwise and hollowed out like a trough. A row of troughs was installed trough up and capped with a row trough down. The overlapping logs kept the rain, wind, and snow out. The Ice Lake post office was opened in 1903 and operated by Robert Brett. This farm settlement boasts rolling farmland, rock piles created by the pioneers, and farmhouses typical of a prosperous era, including several cement homes.

The south road across from Benedict Lumber features a stone

schoolhouse and the unique Rock Shop and Lapidary, where one can purchase polished island fieldstone, a popular souvenir.

At the sharp right turn, two handsome red frame barns illustrate the evolution in barn construction; the smaller one was built in 1923 and the larger one in 1948. On the south side of the road is Ice Lake. The road crosses part of it by causeway. On the right, at the end of the causeway, is the site of the Runnalls homestead. Newlyweds William Nelson Runnalls and Catherine Ann Rowe homesteaded here in 1873, and held the customary 'stumping bee.' The neighbourhood men and their oxen pulled stumps from the land and dragged away the logs, while the women held a quilting bee. Catherine Runnalls bore five sons before moving west to Barrie Island in 1884. The remains of the Runnalls site, a few Lombardy poplars and an old foundation, may still be seen on the hill.

A farmstead on the right features a beautiful wood-frame silo. The Montgomerys' solid frame barn and silo, still in use, are a tribute to their builder, Chris Montgomery, who had settled here by 1881.

Most non-native settlers came here to farm. In the 1880s wheat was a popular commodity. The next decade saw a shift to oats and hay. By the turn of the century, island farmers were shipping cattle and lambs by the thousands, as well as tons of wool. In the 1920s turkeys were introduced, largely to control the island grasshoppers; however, turkeys quickly became a popular agricultural product throughout the province. Farmers fought to keep on top of the industry with innovations like incubators and the Gore Bay turkey eviscerating plant. Unfortunately, rising costs curtailed this industry in the mid-1960s.

The Ice Lake area has a number of the island's 175 drumlins, according to L.J. Chapman and D.F. Putnam in *The Physiography of Southern Ontario*. Drumlins, a Celtic word for little hills, are oval mounds of glacial till, souvenirs of our glacial age. The angle of these drumlins indicates the direction of travel of the glacier which formed them. After Ice Lake you cross a large and fertile agricultural plain.

Between Ice Lake and Gore Bay is an outcropping of Manitoulin dolomite rock. Dolomite is a Silurian limestone which was deposited in an ancient sea 425 million years ago on top of a bed of softer Ordovician limestone, deposited about 25 million years earlier. This smooth, polished rock can be cut in slabs for hearths and mantels. Dolomite can also be seen at Cup and Saucer Hill.

Highway 542 South passes through the communities of Advance and Long Bay. The Advance post office opened in 1908, with William Gilroy as postmaster. Long Bay's post office opened in 1884, with Robert Gamey as postmaster. One year later R. McKeown of the Long Bay sawmill boasted that the community was booming and needed a hotel. Robert Gamey became Manitoulin's first member of provincial parliament in 1902. He held the position until his death in 1917. Beniah Bowman, a Long Bay farmer and Mennonite lay minister, replaced Gamey in a by-election in 1918. Bowman, the first member of the United Farmers of Ontario ever elected, is remembered for his island road building program in the 1920s.

Gore Bay

At the intersection of Highways 542 and 540 turn north into Gore Bay, the judicial seat of the island. Gore Bay is a picturesque spot with the island's best-preserved residential neighbourhood and a beautiful shoreside boardwalk. Park your car at the marina to explore the town on foot. Gore Bay's highlights include the commercial district, museum, lighthouse, and east bluff lookout. This is also a good spot to purchase supplies for additional touring.

Gore Bay and the limestone cliff–lined North Channel inlet on which it is situated were named either for the tapering gore which runs inland to form this bay, or for the steamer *Gore* which called at island ports between 1838 and 1853 and was once trapped here during a winter storm. Captain Henry Bayfield, who charted Lake Huron and published the area's first accurate map in 1830, named this bay Janet Cove. The native name for this spot was Pashkdinong, or 'barren hill,' which gives some idea of what the spot must have looked like more than a hundred years ago. Today the town is nestled between two tree-covered bluffs. The west bluff rises gently to farmland while the east bluff climbs abruptly for 252 m (825 feet).

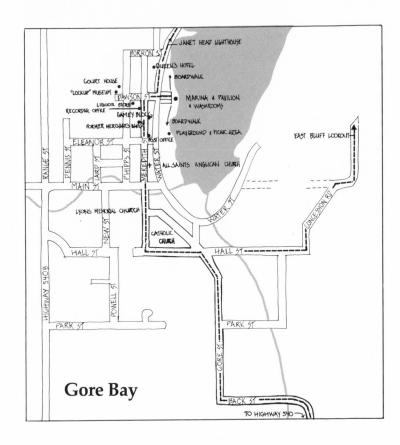

Gore Bay

The Gore Bay harbour

Willard Hall, born in New Brunswick in 1819, came to Gore Bay via Collingwood in 1869 on the steamer *Waubano*. He returned the following year with his wife, Jane Dinsmore, and their eight children. Kagawong pioneer and sailboat operator Luke Chatreau provided the transportation. About the same time Ned Saunders arrived in his sailboat and settled on the shore, where he built a small dugout. By about 1877 Ned decided the town was becoming too crowded and moved west to Elizabeth Bay and later to the remote south shore on Misery Bay. Ned (Edwin) Saunders (1822–95), born and educated in Crediton, England, came with his family to Canada in 1849. Ned was a bachelor, scholar, and musician who preferred to live alone with nature in as remote a setting as possible. It appears

A postcard of Gore Bay (c 1930)

Ned's love of the land and nature was shared by at least one other member of his family, brother William, who made an extended visit to Ned's home in 1880. William Saunders (1836–1914) was an internationally noted pharmacist, naturalist, and agriculturalist.

The next four settlers arrived when Gordon Township was surveyed between 1871 and 1872. They were William McKeown, James M. Fraser, John Hector McQuarrie, and James M. Thorburn. The last three set out from Caledonia, Ontario, and were related through marriage. William McKeown built a small dock for settlers and freight. In 1872 Robert Thorburn (1839–1924) and his family settled here. He opened Gore Bay's first store the following year on the west side of the bay. Thorburn was known as Nitchi (friend) Thorburn by his native neighbours and customers, one of whom, John Moquam (Otchonomequom), lived in a wigwam near the store. As more settlers arrived John Moquam moved west to Lake Wolsey. John McQuarrie's *The Early Years of Gore Bay* is a good source of information on Gore Bay's first settlers.

The Gore Bay town plot was surveyed in August 1875 and the first lot was sold in August 1876. The first area to be settled was in the vicinity of Water Street, near Borron Street; the settlement gradually moved southwest into the present downtown. In 1874 Gore Bay became the fourth location on the island to have a post office, an official recognition of a settlement. By 1880 it had a sawmill, small grist mill, wharves, stores, houses, and a hotel. According to the *Ontario Gazetteer and Business Directory* of 1884–5, Gore Bay was a flourishing village of six hundred people with four churches, a school, saw, shingle, and flour mills, five stores, and three hotels. When the District of Manitoulin was formed, separating the island from the jurisdiction of Algoma, there was a great controversy over where the judicial seat should be located. A plebiscite was held and Gore Bay was selected in 1889. Both Little Current and Manitowaning competed for this honour. According to the *Manitoulin Expositor* (based in Manitowaning and possibly biased), Little Current and Manitowaning split the eastern vote, so Gore Bay won. By the time it was incorporated as a town on 7 April 1890 Gore Bay was the successful centre of a large farming community, as well as a shipping and lumbering town. The town's first council included J. Russell McGregor as mayor, J.S. Hawkins as town clerk, and blacksmiths George Young and George Porter, plasterer George Strain, hotel keeper H.L. McLean, tinsmith John Baxter, and merchant Peter Anderson as council members.

The boardwalk south leads to a picnic area and playground. Across the street is the Municipal Building and Library, which was opened on 7 April 1990 to mark the centennial of the incorporation of Gore Bay. The first town library was established in 1891 as a Mechanics Institute. Smith Memorial Park was donated by Doug Smith in memory of his parents, Bill and Rita Smith, and his grandfather Fred Smith. The Smiths have been local entrepreneurs since 1898 when 23-year-old Fred Smith opened a creamery. A short time later he opened a grocery store. Fred is remembered for quietly filling grocery orders on credit during the Depression in the 1930s. If you head in the opposite direction on the boardwalk, past the marina, you will see the former Queen's Hotel on Water Street. This, Gore Bay's third hotel, was built in 1888 by Hector Lachlan McLean. Hotels and boarding houses were a necessity in new communities. By 1880 the island had nine licensed hotels, including two in Gore Bay.

The boardwalk was the site of a citizens' parade of history during the town's centennial celebrations in 1990.

Gore Bay's first saw and grist mills were built on the shore in 1877 by William F. McRae.

Walk up Borron Street from the waterfront and turn left onto Meredith Street, which contains some fine examples of Gore Bay's residential architecture. Notice how the east and west sides of Meredith Street are on different levels or terraces, which were created by ancient shorelines. If time permits you may enjoy wandering through other residential streets.

To the right, on Dawson Street, stand two of the island's outstanding architectural works, the court-house and the Gore Bay Museum. The latter is operated by the Western Manitoulin Historical Society. The museum has displays of pioneer household and farm equipment as well as dental tools, a pioneer buggy, a fire engine, and relics of the area's many shipwrecks, including artefacts reputed to be from La Salle's *Griffon*. The Gore Bay

The court-house was designed in 1889 by Kivas Tully, one of the most talented architects of the period.

Museum, open daily from June to September, was originally the town's jail, or 'lockup' as it was known in those days. It was completed in October 1879 by the Law Building Company of Meaford, Ontario. During the 1879 construction season seventeen other town buildings were erected. The lockup stood out, even then, because of its cliffside location, stone construction, and size. William Edwin Saunders (son of William Saunders), who visited the town in 1880, noted in his journal: 'Gore Bay's lockup – a gigantic building.' The only other structures to impress him were the lighthouse and the Ocean House Hotel where he stayed. The first keeper of the lockup was Alex Thorburn. This was the island's third lockup: both Manitowaning and Little Current received Ontario Department of Public Works lockups in 1878.

The court-house was designed by the Ontario Department of Public Works' chief architect, Kivas Tully, one of the most talented Canadian architects of his period. The construction contract was awarded in June 1889 to George Ball of Barrie Island for $5,680. The original two-storey stone structure's beauty lies in its simplicity. It has a straightforward gabled roof facing the front and a central entry decorated with a fanlight and wood pilasters. Additions to the building were made in 1901 and 1924.

Return down the hill and continue through downtown on Meredith Street. Most of Gore Bay's downtown was razed by a fire in 1908 in which fifteen businesses and eight dwellings were destroyed. Two of the most noteworthy buildings sit opposite each other: the Credit Union and the Gamey Block. The three-storey brick Gamey Block was built in 1907, gutted by fire in 1908, and immediately restored. It was owned by Robert Gamey, Manitoulin's first member of the provincial parliament. He was elected in 1902 and remained in office until his death in 1917. Gamey had come to the island in 1877 with his family, headed by his father, Joseph. They settled southwest of Gore Bay in Campbell Township, where Robert began to sell insurance. His career choice exposed him to the majority of islanders and their territory, and made him a well-known candidate for political office when Algoma received its parliamentary seat. The Gamey Block was constructed by a local contractor, George Strain, who hired brick masons from Toronto as none were to be found on Manitoulin. The third floor was a popular spot in the early days. At the 'Gamey Hall' people attended silent movies, meetings, concerts, dances, and box socials. The second floor has always contained offices and apartments, while the first has been reserved for shops.

Another of George Strain's masonry construction projects, the former Merchants Bank, now the Espanola and District Credit Union, is located across the street. The Merchants Bank (later the Bank of Montreal) opened the second of their island locations in Gore Bay in 1903. They constructed this building in 1922 and occupied it until the Bank of Montreal building was erected down the street. The town's first bank was established by Messrs Hurst and Burke in 1898, across the street from the present Bank of Montreal.

George Strain Sr was responsible for many island buildings. He was born in Flesherton, Ontario, in 1858, and came to Mani-

Janet Head lighthouse is the island's second oldest lighthouse.

toulin in 1883, settling in Gore Bay in 1889. His contracts include Turner's store and the Mansion House in Little Current and the Merchants Bank, Gamey Block, court-house, and numerous residences in Gore Bay.

The Community Hall was built in 1927 by local mason Stewart Clarke. Clarke was born in England in 1853 and by the turn of the century resided in Gore Bay with his wife, Sarah, and their children. The Gore Bay post office was designed in 1930 by the federal Department of Public Works to house postal, customs, and Indian agency services. Between 1929 and 1935 Public Works built about thirty small federal buildings in Canada, using only a few basic styles. Gore Bay was the first to receive the new side-entrance plan. The Gore Bay building was to be

Gore Bay as seen from the East Bluff lookout

clad in limestone quarried a few kilometres away, but brick was substituted before construction began. Some interesting design features include the truncated hipped roof, a side entrance with projecting front topped with a parapeted gable, and the parapeted dormer windows on the upper level.

The *Manitoulin Guide*, the island's first newspaper, was started in Gore Bay by S.P. Jackson in October 1877. A few months later the *Enterprise* was begun by Harry Mander. The *Algoma Conservator and Manitoulin Outlook* and the *Manitoulin Reformer* soon followed. In 1908 the *Manitoulin Recorder* was created through the amalgamation of the *Manitoulin Guide* and the *Enterprise*. The *Manitoulin Recorder* is still publishing; its affiliated monthly publication *Through the Years* is renowned for its local history articles. Current and back issues of *Through the Years* may be purchased at the *Recorder* office downtown.

The present Stedman's store was formerly the Stone Block,

This unique stone silo sits a few kilometres south of Gore Bay.

which managed to escape the 1908 fire. The inferno, which broke out where the Community Hall stands today, destroyed everything between here and the Gamey Block, then spread across the street. Originally there were three separate businesses on the Stone Block's ground floor.

All Saints Anglican Church was built in 1882 on property donated by H.B. Hunt, the proprietor of the Ocean House Hotel. This neat white wooden Gothic Revival-style church features pointed windows, a raised entry porch, and a belfry, added in 1884. Farther south, the Blacksmith Square gift shop was built in 1902 by William Griffith as a blacksmith shop. Across the street, behind the garage, stands Manitoulin Lodge, a residence for seniors. Built in 1923 as the Public and Continuation School by the McLarty Brothers of Sault Ste Marie, it was renamed C.C. McLean School in 1963 after a long-time local teacher.

Lyons Memorial Church, a pretty stone building designed in the popular Gothic Revival style, was completed in 1886 as Lyons Methodist. It is named for the Rev. Almon P. Lyons, who founded the Wesleyan Methodist congregation here in 1880. In

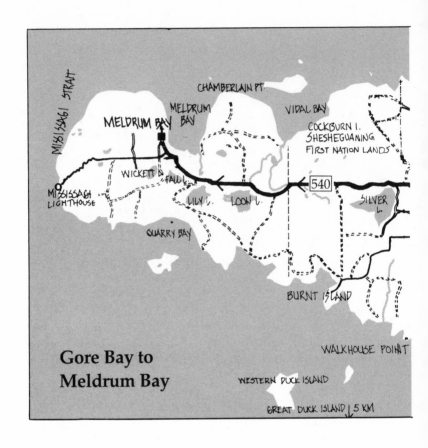

Gore Bay to Meldrum Bay

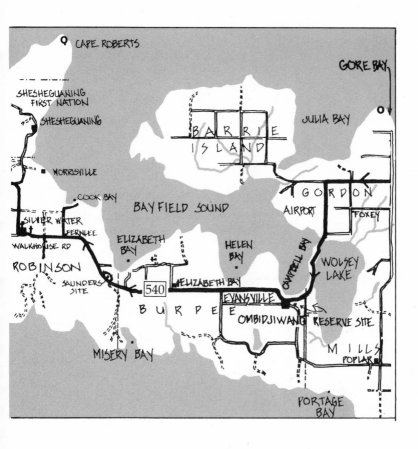

1917 Gore Bay's Methodist and Presbyterian congregations joined to form the Union Church because of wartime financial difficulties. The Methodist church building and the Presbyterian manse were retained. The church was renamed Lyons United in 1925, when the national United Church of Canada was formed. The adjoining hall was built in 1955 in memory of Bob Robinson, the local Sunday school superintendent.

In 1909 J. Russell McGregor, the proud owner of Gore Bay's first automobile, a McLaughlin Carriage Company vehicle, made what is believed to be the first automobile tour of Manitoulin. He visited Little Current, Manitowaning, Providence Bay, and returned to Gore Bay. An easy 35 km drive today, McGregor's trip as far as Providence Bay took at least two hours. This thrilling tour was recalled by witnesses to the event some seventy years later. McGregor's Tudhope was acquired and restored by Ed Burt of Ice Lake and is a popular attraction at local car rallies.

After exploring the town on foot, drive north on Water Street to Janet Head lighthouse. The island's second oldest lighthouse was completed in October 1879 by contractor Carmichael and local mason Jones. The foundation is made of stone and sand from nearby Helen's Bay. It is a white square wooden building 12 m (40 feet) high, with an attached dwelling. The light was designed to be visible for almost 18 km (11 miles). Janet Head Point is believed to be named for a daughter of Captain Bayfield, who surveyed Lake Huron from the ship *Recovery* in 1817–22. Robert Boyter (1838–95) was the first lighthouse keeper. He was born in Pittenweem, Scotland, and emigrated to Thornbury, Ontario, around 1868. His wife, Isabella, died tragically in the winter of 1885: she succumbed to exposure after travelling over the ice from Gore Bay to accompany a son to the town of Spanish on the North Shore. The tragedy was deepened when the team which set out to retrieve her body was lost in a blizzard, resulting in a young girl's death by exposure and the amputation of two young men's feet. The event was a telling example of the perils of winter travel in this district only a hundred years ago.

The east bluff is a worthwhile stop for a panoramic view of the bay. To reach the lookout go south on Meredith Street; turn left onto Hall Street and follow Hall as it jogs across Gore Street. Follow the concession road up the hill, turn right at the T-intersection, then follow the road as it turns left. Here you have a spectacular view of Gore Bay town and waterfront, as well as the surrounding farmland. From here continue back down the bluff and turn left onto Gore Street.

Highway 540B passes the home of Manitoulin Transport Inc., founded in 1960 by Doug Smith, whose family has been involved in businesses in Gore Bay since 1898. Manitoulin Transport is one of the island's largest employers, its trucks moving goods throughout the province.

Gore Bay to Meldrum Bay

After exploring Gore Bay, return to Highway 540 west. For an interesting side trip take Poplar Road south for a glimpse of some island farm silos. Just south of Highway 540 is a handsome stone silo built by mason Stewart Clarke of Gore Bay. The farm also has a large frame barn and cement Gothic-style farmhouse. Just ahead on the left are two wooden silos.

The local nine-hole, 100-acre golf course is just southwest of town. Highway 540 west crosses fertile plains, barren grazing land, and a causeway, and passes several ghost ports. For 4.5 km (2.7 miles) the road crosses the grazing plains of Gordon Township, surveyed by Edgar Bray and named Sherborne in August 1871 by the Indian Department. A Sherborne Township already existed elsewhere in Ontario, so in September of that year it was renamed Gordon, apparently for the Hon. James Gordon of Toronto, a member of the Legislative Council from 1845 to 1865. The area is known for its large barns and farmhouses, signs of a successful farming community. The highway temporarily heads south here, though you may continue due west to the Gore Bay airport and Barrie Island. Barrie Island is a great spot for bird watching. Great eagles, sandhill cranes, and even a northern wheatear bird have been spotted here.

Regularly scheduled flights to Toronto and Elliot Lake depart from the Gore Bay airport. Sightseeing trips are available. The airport was constructed by the federal government in 1947. Barrie Island is a low limestone plateau with about two dozen farms. It was surveyed in 1879 by J.W. Fitzgerald, and named for Captain Robert Barrie by Captain Bayfield during his 1817–22 survey of these waters. The post office, opened in 1882, was first operated by Peter Archdekon, a 28-year-old farmer. The mail arrived twice weekly via stage from Gore Bay. The Lattas, who arrived from Shelburne, Ontario, in 1876, settled on the north side of the sharp left turn as you travel from the causeway onto the island. Archibald Latta and his children used their boat to transport people to Barrie Island.

Barrie Island, along with pockets near Sheguiandah, Mindemoya, Providence Bay, and Gore Bay, has some of the island's most fertile land. Two 'century' farms are located in this community, both homesteaded by the Runnalls family. In 1879 William O. Runnalls, with his son William Nelson Runnalls and daughter-in-law Catherine, purchased two 100-acre lots from the Crown for $50 per lot. The Runnalls family moved here in 1884 from Ice Lake. William Nelson Runnalls, from Northumberland County, Ontario, had settled at Ice Lake in 1873 following his marriage to Catherine Ann Rowe. Catherine was the daughter of William Rowe, who settled on Manitoulin in 1869.

The Runnalls' homestead. Photo courtesy of Lewis Runnalls.

When William N. died in 1898, Catherine kept up the farm with the assistance of her five sons, the youngest of whom, Percy, eventually took over the farm after serving in the First World War. Percy, like many island bachelors, married a young woman who had come to teach in the local school. Percy and his wife, Effie Hern, raised five children, one of whom, Lewis Runnalls, took over the farm in 1954 and lives there today. According to Lewis, the farm has always been a self-sufficient mixed operation: Shorthorn cattle were kept for both milk and beef, cream was churned to produce butter for sale, sheep were raised for wool, lambs for sale, horses for transportation and labour, and colts for sale. The Runnalls family appears to have farming in its blood, having successfully worked the land for five generations.

About 2 km (1.2 miles) southeast of the Barrie Island corner on Highway 540 a rural route leads 2 km (1.2 miles) east to Foxey, which was the last rural post office to open on the island,

The Barrie Island community wolfhunt was necessary to protect valuable livestock. Photo courtesy of Lewis Runnalls.

in 1911. It closed in 1937. Foxey school, constructed by mason Stewart Clarke, now houses the Gordon municipal offices. The Philemon Wismer family settled in Foxey in 1879. Son Jacob Wismer was the first postmaster here, and son Joseph Wismer, a photographer, provided a documentary record of island people and places for over four decades.

Observe the unusual vegetation: here you will find bur oak trees in grassy beds on top of limestone.

Heading south from the Barrie Island corner the road travels over a narrow peninsula and onto a causeway known as Indian Point Bridge. The causeway divides Bayfield Sound's Campbell Bay, a passage off the North Channel on the right, from Lake Wolsey, on the left. These waters are obviously named for and by their hydrographic surveyor, Captain Henry Wolsey Bayfield. The native name for this narrows was Ombidjiwang, meaning 'at the place where the water rises.' Lake Wolsey is a popular fishing spot containing northern pike, smallmouth bass, and yellow perch. On the immediate right after the bridge is a small picnic area on Campbell Bay, where you can park, enjoy the view, and visit Ombidjiwang cemetery. The high bluff on the west shore of Campbell Bay is, according to legend, the home of the Paheens, or little people. An Ombidjiwang medicine man, Jim Poquam (Bai-gum-quoum), was said to be able to see the Paheens, who resided in the rocks of the bluff, and whose appearances were portents of misfortune.

This is the former Ombidjiwang Reserve No. 21. Like all island reserves, it was created to relocate the natives after the island was opened for general settlement. The Ombidjiwang were non-Christian natives, mainly Odawa and some Ojibwe, numbering about forty-three persons by 1846. By 1870, 32 persons belonged to this band. They retained a traditional lifestyle, largely untouched by schools or religion. According to the 1901 census, five families (twenty persons) resided here; however, the group dispersed over the next few decades.

The original 290 ha (717 acre) Ombidjiwang camp-site consisted of a number of wigwams on the shore of Lake Wolsey at the foot of the bluff. The wigwams were typical of island native residences in the mid-1800s. They were built by tying a group of poles in a conical shape and then covering them with birchbark

The Campbell Bay bluff is credited by some as the home of the Paheens, or little people.

or cedar bark. The natives later built European settler-style log cabins on top of the bluff where they had previously grown corn. The Ombidjiwang were admired by their neighbours for their elegant canoes and their ability to skilfully manoeuvre the sturdy but delicate craft. The two-person canoes were about 5.5 metres (18 feet) long. They had a frame of split-cedar ribs holding narrow cedar planks. The exterior was covered in one-metre-square birchbark pieces sewn together and sealed with pine gum.

The Ombidjiwang cemetery is located on lot 24, concession 1, Mills Township, south of Indian Point. To visit this peaceful site, park at the causeway picnic area and walk west for five minutes. On the south side of the road a wire gate and large pine trees mark the entrance to the cemetery. The site was donated to the township of Mills in 1952 by Ray Merrylees, and the beautiful stand of pine trees which surrounds it was donated in 1954 by the Ontario Paper Company. The last Ombidjiwang buried here was Johnny Moquam (Endahsoogwameb), who died in 1932. He was the son of Old John Moquam (Otchonomequom). The pink granite boulder which marks Johnny Moquam's grave is the only marker in the cemetery.

Years ago the site had a number of wigwamaces, or board houses, which were placed over the graves. Old John Moquam's grave was the last to receive a traditional wigwamace. According to observations made at Sheguiandah in the nineteenth century, a wigwamace was made of hand-split cedar boards, about 6 or 7 feet long by 3 feet wide, with low walls 6 to 9 inches high that sloped to a peaked roof about 18 inches high. The deceased's axe, bow and arrow, a miniature canoe, a clay pipe, matches, tobacco, a dish of water, dried corn, and maple sugar were placed inside to provision him on his four-day journey to the afterlife. Friends passing the cemetery would place a gift of maple sugar or tobacco inside the structure through the small opening at the west end. This burial tradition was widely practised before the Christianization of the island. In 1952 an amateur historian, Frank A. Myers, studied the location of the Ombidjiwang cemetery and placed Manitoulin's first historic site marker there. Most of our information about this band is from Myers, who interviewed Ombidjiwang descendants and their neighbours in the early 1950s. Much of his research has been reprinted in the December 1983 and August 1986 issues of *Through the Years*, available at the Gore Bay *Recorder* office.

Highway 540 west leads to Evansville, a small farming community. The Colin Campbell family was the first to settle here in 1877. They arrived from Goderich, Ontario, via Sheguiandah, where Colin had worked for the Walker mill, and Gore Bay, where Colin had built the town's first hotel for his son. Colin's son Isaac became the first postmaster in 1884, distributing the weekly mail. Colin built the first sawmill in Evansville in 1886. Evansville was originally located on the shore of Campbell Bay, but it gradually migrated inland. The school was built in 1901, the United Church in 1910, and the Orangemen's Community Hall in 1916. There is a small lookout with a wonderful view over Campbell Bay on the road heading northwest out of Evansville.

The Elizabeth Bay United Church

This is Burpee Township, which was surveyed in 1879 and named for Isaac Burpee of New Brunswick, merchant, entrepreneur, and politician. In 1997 Burpee Township and the unorganized township of Mills formed the Township of Burpee and Mills. An editorial comment in an 1886 edition of the local paper noted that ten of the eighty-odd names on the Burpee provincial voters list were Bailey. William Bailey and his wife, Christina Campbell, and James Bailey and his wife, Catherine, had settled here by 1881.

The road travels through coniferous bush, grazing land, and flat rock plains sprinkled with birch groves. About 3 km (2 miles) west of Evansville, on the north shore, is Helen Bay, believed to have been named by Captain Bayfield for his sister. In 1901 tragedy struck the community when the Helen Bay mill's boiler exploded, killing three men. Elizabeth Bay, to the immediate west, was named for his mother.

Elizabeth Bay's post office opened in 1899. A small sign at the York Church corner directs you to an optional 7 km (4 mile) detour through the community. About 4 km (2.4 miles) northwest of the highway are the Elizabeth Bay United Church, built of fieldstone and limestone, and a former cobblestone school, now a picturesque private residence. James D. Ainslie (1830–1915), his wife, Bridget, and their family emigrated from Roxburghshire, Scotland, in 1871 and moved here in 1878. Gaelic-speaking Scots, they settled about 2.5 km (1.5 miles) west of Elizabeth Bay, where their family cemetery can still be found.

Directly south of Elizabeth Bay is Misery Bay, a provincial nature reserve. This park, for day use only, features twelve different ecological environments including unique limestone pavements and wetlands. A large portion of the park was donated by Eunice and Calvin Sifferd in 1988. Just east of Misery Bay is Mac's Bay Conservation Area where 290 hectares (700 acres) have been provincially designated for traditional use including snowmobiling and picnicking.

Another 4 km (2.4 miles) past Elizabeth Bay the road enters Robinson Township, which was surveyed in 1878 and named after the Hon. John Beverly Robinson, who was lieutenant-governor of Ontario from 1880 to 1887. Robinson is Manitoulin's largest township. It contains 22 concessions and 45 lots, instead of the usual 35 or 36 lots.

About 5 km (3 miles) past Elizabeth Bay, as you turn right, is the former homestead of Ned (Edwin) Saunders. Saunders homesteaded here in a shanty on the shore of Elizabeth Bay to escape the bustle of Gore Bay. He lived here until 1884, when the arrival of more neighbours drove him to Misery Bay on the island's remote south shore. In 1880 Ned was visited by his brother William Saunders, an internationally known agriculturalist and naturalist. The brothers, along with William's children, enjoyed exploring the remote western end of the island together. Though a recluse, Ned was well known and liked by his neighbours.

The road continues northwest, then bends due west again after passing the former post office of Fernlee, which was established in 1901. Take the first right turn for an interesting 3 km (2 mile) detour to an abandoned port. A tree-lined drive through a farm and past birch groves leads to the bay. Beneath a cliff on Cook's Bay, at the western end of Bayfield Sound, is Cook's dock. Although no buildings have survived, the isolated setting of this former fishing station, sawmill, and lumber shipping port is worth a visit. Cook's Bay was named for John and Ellen Cook and their family of six from Holstein, Ontario, who cleared the land. They also built the first dock, which provided access to surrounding homesteads for settlers and supplies. In the mid-1880s fishermen from the Duck Islands south of Manitoulin established a fishing station here. Today the south-shore-based Purvis Brothers operate a fishing boat from the dock. This is a wonderful fishing spot. On a calm day fish can often be seen swimming alongside the dock. Children are practically guaranteed a small catch.

Just past Cook's Bay road is the Walkhouse side-road. This isolated area was settled around 1879. The John and Catherine Duncanson family came in 1882 from Middlesex County, Ontario. They arrived by boat at the Duck Islands fishing station, off the island's south shore, where a small boat was chartered to land them south at Walkhouse Point. The Duncansons and their eight children walked 9 miles to their land along a native path called the Tecumseh Trail. This trail began at Walkhouse Point, about 8 km (5 miles) south of Silver Water on the Lake Huron shore, and wound north through Robinson Township and the Shesheguaning Reserve to the tip of Cape Robert on the North Channel. About 3 km (2 miles) west of Silver Water on the southern tip of Silver Lake, the Wacausia native camp existed around 1850. The Wacausia band abandoned the camp in the 1860s to live on the reserves. According to W.R. Wightman, author of *Forever on the Fringe: Six Studies in the Development of the Manitoulin Island*, the name Walkhouse was probably a corruption of 'Wacausia,' the name of the chief of the small band who used a portage to Walkhouse Bay en route to the fishing grounds at the Duck Islands.

You are approaching the community of Silver Water, where you may turn north to continue to the island's west coast, or detour west and south to visit the Burnt Island fishing station, which sells fresh fish.

St Andrew's United Church, on the north side of Highway

540, was dedicated on 2 July 1899 as St Andrew's Presbyterian. The original white frame church building was replaced in 1999 after 100 years of service.

To the south is Nineteen Lake, named for its location on lot 19, concession 8, Robinson Township. On the west side of the lake, where the highway turns north, is the hamlet of Silver Water, settled around 1878. Its post office opened in 1883 with a twice-weekly service from Gore Bay and Lewis Kemp as postmaster. Kemp's post office and store were located about 3 km northwest in a log house he built in 1878 near the Tecumseh Trail. O.M. Thompson and Company (partner William Lloyd of Kagawong) opened a general store here in 1911, an indication of a prospering community. This was once western Manitoulin Island's most important village, a retail centre for the farming district and its two ports. Today the ports, sawmills, and many of the farms have disappeared, although several stores, homes, and a school built in 1912 remain. On the north side of the highway is St Peter's Anglican Church, built in 1897. Before the community's churches were built, Anglicans and Presbyterians both held services in the school; most parishioners attended all services in true community spirit. The first settlers were Henry and Robert Farthing, brothers from Middlesex County, Ontario, George and Henry Smyth from Oxford County, Ontario, and John Edmonds. They travelled by steamer to Gore Bay, by small sailboat to Shesheguaning, then via the Tecumseh Trail to Silver Water.

The John and Margaret Edmonds family settled about 1.5 km (1 mile) west of Silver Water in 1879. They later discovered that the 'clearing' on which they built their house was actually the well-travelled Tecumseh Trail. Natives accustomed to travelling the trail would knock at their front door, visit briefly, and then leave through the back door. Perhaps they hoped to bring bad luck to this roadblock; ordinarily, for good luck, the native custom was to enter and exit through the same door.

For a look at an operating fishing station, drive straight west through Silver Water instead of following the highway north. Two kilometres (1.2 miles) west of town follow the road and causeway to Burnt Island, where the Purvis Brothers established their fishing business in 1882. On 21 March 1877, William

Purvis (1830–1914) received a government appointment as lighthouse keeper on Great Duck Island, located in Lake Huron about 18 km (11 miles) south of Burnt Island. Purvis received an annual salary of $500 as lightkeeper. One of North America's oldest undisturbed sand dune complexes can be found on Great Duck Island.

Purvis also brought his wife, Ann Frost, and their ten children to Great Duck Island; until 1899 they resided on the island during the shipping season and in Gore Bay during the winter. William operated the lighthouse and fished. His five sons started fishing operations in Gore Bay, Providence Bay, Michipicoten Island, and Lake Winnipeg. Three of George Purvis's sons joined forces and incorporated Purvis Brothers in 1946. Most of the whitefish and chubb they catch are shipped to Chicago, Boston, and New York. The trout population was destroyed with the arrival of the sea lamprey via the new Welland Canal in 1934. Visitors are welcome to visit the Purvis Brothers Fishery, and to purchase fresh fish from Monday through Saturday here as well as at other island locations. In 1936 the Purvis Brothers began breeding mink and silver fox, as the diet of these animals consists largely of fish entrails. Their ranch was one of three formerly on the island.

Belanger Bay, part of the QUNO forest lands, is a unique limestone pavement of alvar, which, according to island naturalist Judith Jones, is a community of rare, endemic plants. To date access has been limited.

From Silver Water, Highway 540 continues north. Where the highway bends west, you may detour a few kilometres north to see another abandoned port, Morrisville, and Shesheguaning First Nation. Drive almost 2 km (1.2 miles) down the hill and turn right to a rocky beach where Morrisville post office was established in 1900. In 1911 the post office was relocated 5 km (3 miles) north to Shesheguaning. The Shesheguaning First Nation (Reserve No. 20) and the adjacent Cockburn Island Reserve, or Zhiibaahaasing (the passageway), are located north of here. Father J. Edward O'Flaherty, SJ, who did extensive research on native place names, wrote that Shesheguaning means 'at the place of the rattle' or 'at the place where a rattle was hung,' or, according to some, 'place of the rattlesnakes.'

This last translation often excites visitors, and while rattlesnakes have been reported on Manitoulin – though not confirmed – that translation is considered to be the least likely of the three. The name does signify rattle, but it more likely refers to a musical rattle which, like the drum, was used in ceremonies. This was an Odawa settlement from at least 1839, when Roman Catholic natives came here instead of going to Wikwemikong. Edowishkosh, son of J.B. Assiginack (Chief Blackbird), settled here with his family. By 1856 there were 32 Anglican and 31 Catholic parishioners. In 1865 the 126 natives (33 families) actively petitioned the government for the location to remain their permanent reserve. The official boundary was established in 1879 during the island survey, and consisted of 1,865 ha (4,606 acres). The Zhiibaahaasing community (population 35) has the world's largest peace pipe and dream catcher on display. The community's powwows are popular attractions.

The northernmost tip of land is Cape Robert. A lighthouse was built here in 1885, at the same time as the one at Manitowaning on the east coast. The white square wood tower with an attached dwelling had a light 13 metres (46 feet) above the bay and was visible for 20 km (12 miles).

Seven kilometres (4 miles) west of the Shesheguaning road a trail leads north to the site of the Shesheguaning native camp. The band, of around a dozen persons, lived on the western shore of Vidal Bay from about the mid-1840s to the mid-1860s. According to W.R. Wightman, the Ontario Paper Company purchased about 80,000 acres in this vicinity on western Manitoulin in 1947. While undertaking a minimal harvest, they immediately began reforestation, allowing for extended regrowth. They also encouraged other forest owners to do the same. Declining prices, demand, and production ultimately forced the idea of regrowth on foresters across the entire island. Manitoulin's forests finally received a much deserved rest, after being harvested or burned almost continually since settlement began.

Continuing west the road enters Dawson, Manitoulin's most westerly township. Established in 1878, it is believed to be named for Simon J. Dawson, surveyor, engineer, and legislator. He was elected to the Ontario legislature in 1874 and represented this riding in the House of Commons from 1878 to 1891.

Dawson township bustled in the early 1890s with farming, fishing, logging, and quarrying. Miners from Michigan quarried rock for the Sault Ste Marie Canada Ship Canal, which opened in 1895.

About 14 km (9 miles) west of Silver Water, on Vidal Bay on the north shore, is another former native camp-site. Early settlers discovered a native burial ground at the mouth of Maple Lake Creek.

After winding and rolling over about 26 km (16 miles) of terrain from Silver Water, the highway arrives at beautiful Macrae Cove on Meldrum Bay. The bay is surrounded by steep forested hills; its hamlet is located on the west shore. Meldrum Bay seems little altered since it was settled 110 years ago, and currently contains an inn, store, museum, church, marina, and numerous residences.

Parking is available between the marina and the inn. The campground and the Meldrum Bay Inn are fine starting points for a tour of the community. Macrae Cove, to the right, is backed by a small hillside clearing with an old log cabin. To the left is Newberry Cove. The bay ends at Chamberlain Point. The tiny island to the far left is Batture.

The Meldrum Bay Inn's dining rooms feature good home cooking and a chance to meet locals as well as boaters, and the accommodations (seven rooms with a shared bathroom) are comfortable. The restaurant at the Mississagi Strait lighthouse is another dining option. It also provides good food, all the more welcome after the additional 10 km (6 mile) excursion over rough roads.

Meldrum Bay was named and charted as 'Mildram Bay' by Captain Henry Bayfield during his hydrographic survey of 1817–22. The first settlers arrived in 1876, the same year J.W. Fitzgerald commenced surveying Dawson Township. Meldrum Bay has survived as a farming, fishing, and lumbering port. The post office opened in 1880, managed by John Switzer for a few months, then by Richard Cundle, a 23-year-old Ontario-born millhand. Humphrey May brought the mail here by horse and sleigh during the winters. He left Little Current at 6 a.m., and stopped at Kagawong, Gore Bay, Barrie Island, Cook's dock, Silver Water, and usually arrived at Meldrum Bay at midnight.

May was born in 1844 at Manitowaning where his father was employed by the government, and is said to have been the first child born on Manitoulin to non-native settlers. However, Frances Mary Brough DuMoulin (1839–1931), daughter of missionary C.C. Brough, may rightfully claim that distinction.

In 1880 the first sawmill was built and operated by the town's first storekeeper, William Switzer, who sold it two years later. The mill had numerous owners before 1901, when the Manitoulin Ranch and Lumber Company opened a lumber, shingle, and lath sawmill. This company, based in Walkerville, Ontario, operated until 1914, and employed about a hundred men. During the boom period the town boasted stores and boarding houses. In 1919 Art Wickett built a sawmill near the present location of the Department of Transportation and Communication depot. Beginning around 1921 the sawmill produced fish boxes. By the 1930s the town was dubbed Fish Box Bay because of the large number of boxes stacked awaiting shipment. The sawmill burned in 1951, and its rusting remains can be seen near the water.

Commercial fishing was started around 1897 by J.P. Mac-Donald, the son of the Mississagi Island lighthouse keeper. Mac-Donald was joined by Joseph (Joe) Millman (1876–1963), with whom he had fished at Pewpork and Cockburn islands. Joe set up his own fish business with Jack Keen around 1902 and built his own net shed in 1907. This net shed is now a museum and features artefacts from the fishing and lumbering trades, shipwrecks, and community life. Commercial fishing continued until about 1942, when the sea lamprey and overfishing destroyed the trout population. Mississagi Strait salmon fishermen still dock here.

In 1918 Meldrum Bay consisted of twenty-five farmers, eleven fishermen, thirty-five housekeepers, and eleven other adults, plus children. It was quite a sizeable settlement, considering its remote location.

Many ships called here during the shipping era. Several met with misfortune: the *John J. Long* burned at the wharf on 3 September 1901, and the tug *Windslow*, owned by Reed Wrecking Co., burned in 1910. The *John J. Long*'s short history of death and rebirth was not unusual for vessels on these waters. Built in

1894 in Collingwood, it burned and sank in 1901 in Meldrum Bay, but its hull and machinery were salvaged and rebuilt in Wiarton into a longer, larger vessel. In 1903 the ship was purchased in Goderich by Little Current's premier shipping/mercantile family, the Sims brothers, who renamed it the *Iroquois*. The *Iroquois* served North Shore and Manitoulin ports until 1908, when it sank off the town of Spanish on the North Shore.

From 1947 to 1968 the ferry *Normac* operated between Meldrum Bay and Blind River, directly north on the North Shore of Lake Huron. By 1964 it ran this two-hour trip twice daily in addition to its weekly service to Cockburn Island.

The Outfitter store has been in operation since 1900, when it was run by Thomas Falls, the postmaster. The Meldrum Bay Inn, originally James Fitzpatrick's Grand Manitoulin Hotel, has been sheltering visitors since about 1906. Fitzpatrick sold out within a decade of opening, claiming the government's Temperance Act drastically reduced his profits. Up the hill from the marina are the community's church and hall. In 1888 the first school was built where the community hall now stands. The hall was built in 1932 by Stewart Clarke, a Gore Bay mason. The United Church was built in 1920.

From Meldrum Bay, the adventurous tourist may continue west to the Mississagi Strait lighthouse, which is open in summer beginning the long weekend in May. This wonderful, remote lighthouse is at the end of a 10 km (6 mile) road, the last 5 km (3 miles) of which is narrow, winding, and rough. Leave Meldrum Bay and turn west for the lighthouse. The first 5 km (3 miles) runs through rolling farmland. About 1 km (0.6 miles) southwest of Highway 540, between Wickett and Falls lakes, is a bird sanctuary and wildlife preserve. Wickett Lake is named for George Wickett, who settled in the general vicinity in 1879, and on this land around 1882. George purchased this land from the William Thorburn family, which was relocating to 'civilization' in Gore Bay, where they hoped to have access to a doctor, having recently lost a child to diphtheria. At the west end of the lake was a small native camp in the late 1870s. Falls Lake was named for Thomas Falls, an Ontario-born Irishman who farmed here with his family.

A further 2 km (1.2 miles) lead to School Section No. 1, a

Mississagi Strait lighthouse was first lit in 1873.

cement block building built in 1927. This schoolhouse replaced one built here in 1897 at the centre of the school section, replacing the township's first school, built in Meldrum Bay in 1888. Behind the school is the site of a native camp which existed in the 1870s and 1880s. Next is the community cemetery on the south side, and the former Ball homestead. Hector Ball, his son Jim, and their wives moved here in 1879 from Brant County, Ontario. Their prized possessions included several feather beds, no doubt a much-envied comfort, as well as a large selection of carpentry tools and chinaware. One kilometre past the cemetery is a square log pioneer cabin and a unique cellar whose triangular fieldstone walls can be seen in the field to the west.

The highway-grade pavement ends after 5 km (3 miles). Continue past a sign that proclaims 'Private road, use at own risk.' The rough winding route has become very popular in recent years, and motorists may have to pull over to the side several times to allow others to pass. The pavement ends at a quarry 2 km (1.2 miles) farther on and turns into loose gravel over

Mississagi Strait lighthouse today

the last 2.6 km (1.5 miles) to the lighthouse. The quarry here is the only Canadian operation on the Great Lakes producing metallurgical-grade dolostone. In 1995 over three million tons of various grades of dolomite were quarried and shipped to Montreal, Chicago, and other ports. About five dozen people are employed at this quarry. One look at the rugged, isolated shoreline tells why a lighthouse was needed.

Mississagi Strait lighthouse was built and first lit in 1873 on the western tip of the island to guard the treacherous Mississagi Strait, whose magnetic shoal has caused many shipwrecks. As early as 1828, Captain Henry Bayfield's charts indicated the Strait of Mississauga and its 'magnetic reefs.' The lighthouse stands 8.5 metres (28 feet) high with a white square wooden tower and attached dwelling. The first lighthouse keeper was John Miller. His supplies were delivered twice yearly via a dirt trail. Having just travelled the modern version of this route, one can easily understand why supplies arrived so infrequently. The lighthouse and foghorn building are now a museum; an auto-

View south from the lantern of the lighthouse

mated beacon a few metres north has assumed the lighthouse's
original function.

The site also features a restaurant, a campground, and activi-
ties such as hiking, swimming, diving, and fishing. The Niagara
Escarpment, which stretches across Manitoulin, dips below
Lake Huron at this point.

Many people believe the remains of an ancient ship found on
this shore belong to La Salle's *Griffon*. René-Robert Cavalier
Sieur de La Salle, commandant of Fort Frontenac and a fur
trader, had obtained a commission from King Louis XIV to
explore and claim the Mississippi River for France. The *Griffon*
was built to carry the expedition across the Great Lakes and was
the first commercial vessel to venture there. Thirty-four men in
the 60-foot, 45-tonne ship set sail above Niagara Falls in August
1679. The *Griffon* was bound for Detroit, St Ignace, and Green
Bay, Michigan, where she anchored to take on a load of beaver

pelts. La Salle sent the ship with her cargo of furs back to Niagara for the expedition's financial backers while he and another small crew made their way south. The *Griffon* disappeared during a severe storm on 18 September 1679, and never reached her destination. The Mississagi Wreck, discovered by pioneers in 1879, has long been the leading candidate for the *Griffon* (although recent theories suggest the ship never made it out of Lake Michigan).

From the upper level of the lighthouse the ghost township of Cockburn Island is visible. By 1878, a small community had settled around Tolsmaville fishing station on Cockburn's northeastern bay, where S.F. (Zebe) Tolsma operated a general store, fishing, and tugboat operation. Tolsma, a fisherman from Cheboygan, Michigan, lived here until 1884. In 1879 Cockburn Island was surveyed and leased for timbering. A reserve was established for natives from Shesheguaning. It comprised 340 ha (840 acres) and contained from thirty to sixty residents before 1900. Cockburn's development was based on fishing, farming, and forestry. It became a small but bustling port, with steamboats stopping thrice weekly to load wood ties, telegraph poles, and cedar posts. The land office was moved here from Gore Bay in 1879; its agent looked after all of western and central Manitoulin, but the task proved difficult from Cockburn Island and the land office was returned to Gore Bay in 1892. A post office was opened in 1880 with the local Indian land agent, Benjamin Ross, as postmaster. Cockburn's isolation eventually caused its downfall: while the rest of Manitoulin gained road and rail access, Cockburn remained dependent on steamers to deliver and pick up its goods. As recently as 1964 the ferry *Normac* made weekly trips here from Meldrum Bay. When regular service was suspended the remaining residents left. The former settlement, considered by some a ghost town, now perks up in summer with seasonal residents. Much of the actual village remains, though the buildings are weathered and vacant. The former Cockburn Island Indian Reserve is being revived and rebuilt by descendants of the community. Cockburn Island First Nation renamed itself Zhiibaahaasing or 'the passageway' in 1998.

Retrace your steps at least as far as Evansville, where you

may choose to return by the same route or travel southeast on the Southern Route to Providence Bay or South Baymouth. Should you decide to return via the same route you may be pleasantly surprised by the coastal view, a completely different vista than was enjoyed travelling west.

NINE

The Southern Route
(Tour 2)

Evansville to South Baymouth

This tour follows the 4,000-year-old shoreline of Lake Nipissing, which lay about 1.5 km (1 mile) inland from Manitoulin's south shore. Lake Nipissing was one of several lakes which resulted from the melt-water of the glaciers as they retreated after the last Ice Age. According to *Legacy: The Natural History of Ontario*, by John Theberge, Lake Nipissing was formed about 8,700 years ago and lasted until about 6,000 years ago. The formation of the present Great Lakes occurred 2,000 years later. The tour passes through farming country and several small villages to the island's longest sand beach, past sand dunes and mill sites, and ends at the southeastern ferry port of South Baymouth.

After Evansville take the south road just before Indian Point Bridge; it is the last road on the right, and begins with a sharp right turn up a hill. At the top of this hill, overlooking the bay, is a camping park with a clifftop view of Campbell Bay on Bayfield Sound. The road borders two townships, Burpee to the west and Mills to the east. Mills was surveyed in 1878, ten months after the first settlers arrived, and was named for the Hon. David Mills.

The road bends east here. On the immediate left is Colville's Woolly Harvest farm, an interesting stop for knitting enthusiasts. A unique island operation, Woolly Harvest is owned by

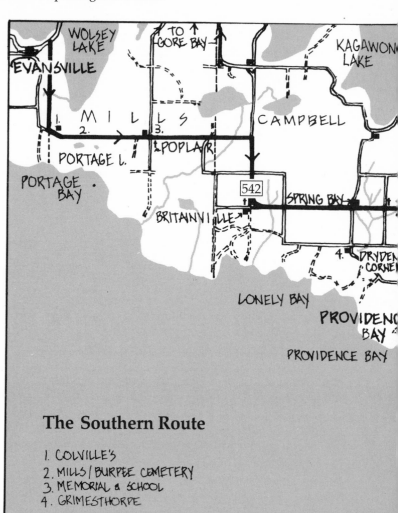

The Southern Route

1. COLVILLE'S
2. MILLS / BURPEE CEMETERY
3. MEMORIAL & SCHOOL
4. GRIMESTHORPE

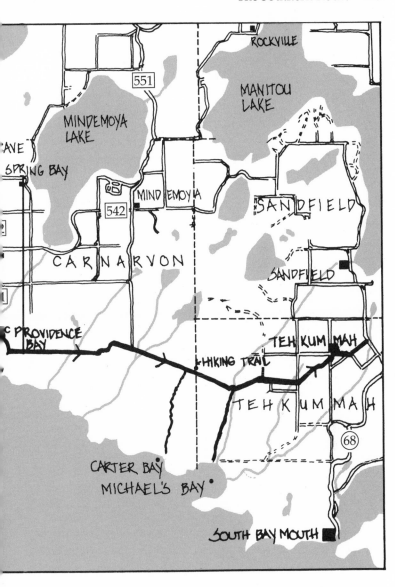

Debby and Bill Colville and their children. This family of sheep farmers shear fleece and dye the wool. The Colville family settled here in 1987 and have been perfecting their craft ever since. The public is invited to visit the farm, view the all-natural process, and purchase the product right at the source.

Watch closely on the right for the sandbanks area, composed of sand dunes and a coniferous forest. High on a hillside to the left is the Mills/Burpee Cemetery. The site is one of two which claim the distinction of being the narrowest point on the island. Technically, a spot between Elizabeth Bay and Misery Bay is the narrowest, but some islanders ignore the Indian Point Causeway and consider Campbell Bay and Lake Wolsey to be continuous water, making this spot, between the south end of Wolsey and Lake Huron 2 km (1.2 miles) to the south, the narrowest on the island. Wolsey and Lake Huron are, in fact, separated by the small Portage Lake. The area has long been known as 'the Portage.' By the 1840s it was part of a trail and inland water route used by the native bands to connect camps around the island. It was also used by natives living on the North Shore of Lake Huron to reach the Duck Islands fishing grounds to the southwest. From the south shore's Portage Bay it is less than a 1 km (0.6 mile) portage overland to Portage Lake, then a 1.5 km (1 mile) portage to Lake Wolsey, and from there easy access to camps both west and east via Bayfield Sound. Learning from their native neighbours, many pioneers used this route to reach their land.

The former homesteads of the area's first settlers are next to the cemetery. George Gallagher settled on the west side of the present cemetery in July 1877, Samuel Ireton settled on the east side of the cemetery shortly after, and Edward Noland claimed the next lot east of Ireton's in August 1877. Gallagher was a New Brunswick–born Irishman who finally reached 'the Portage' via Grey County, Ontario, Sheguiandah, and Gore Bay. He was accompanied by his brother-in-law John B. Baker, who returned the following year with his family and purchased Samuel Ireton's homestead. The third settler, Edward Noland, brought his wife, Jane, his son, and a yoke of oxen. According to George B. Abrey, who surveyed the district in 1878, fifteen persons homesteaded during the first ten months of settlement, but only four – Gallagher, Noland, P.Y. Smith, and John Scott – remained long enough to patent their land.

The next hamlet is Poplar, which was settled around 1877 for the timber in the area. Unlike most early island settlements, it had no source of water-power. While it may seem isolated, it is actually only 16 km (10 miles) south of Gore Bay. Poplar's post office opened in 1884 with Thomas Sides, a 60-year-old Ontario-born Irish farmer and father of seven, as the first postmaster. At the range road intersection is the Poplar War Memorial, built in recognition of Poplar's large number of First World War soldiers, more per capita than any other community in Canada. Unveiled on 31 August 1924, it was dedicated to Mills Township soldiers. Next to the memorial is School Section No. 1 Mills school. The original school had been established in 1881 in a temporary shanty. In 1883 this lot was purchased from Thomas Sides, who built a log school building. The present school was built by W.E. George in 1907 for just under $1,000. In 1875, nine years after Manitoulin's land sales had begun, there were four schoolhouses on the island. Three were in Assiginack Township and one was at Michael's Bay. By 1879 there were 24 schools. In 1883 the local newspaper proudly announced that the 'great majority of our children are not over two miles to the schoolhouse,' and projected 30 schools by year's end. Across the street is the well-kept Mills United Church. This church was built in 1892 as Mills Presbyterian on one-quarter acre of land donated by James McKenzie. A centennial celebration was held in July 1992. The area's first saw-mill was opened in 1886 by John Scott, whose descendants carried on the operation well into this century. John Scott, Marie (Paddock), and son Frederick arrived in Gore Bay in 1875 on the steamer *Silver Spray*. A few years later the family moved to their mill site. The water-powered sawmill cut lumber, cedar shingles, and wood for fish boxes.

About 4 km (2.4 miles) past Poplar the road enters Campbell Township. It was surveyed in 1867 and named for Sir Alexander Campbell, who was commissioner of Crown Lands from 1864 to 1867 and lieutenant-governor of Ontario from 1887 to 1892. In 1998 Campbell, Carnarvon, and Sandfield townships combined to form the Township of Central Manitoulin.

The eastbound road ends at Highway 542. Turn right and follow the highway for 4 km (2.4 miles) as it curves east again at Britainville. William McCormick was Britainville's only postmaster, from 1892 to 1936. William was born around 1855 in Ireland and by 1891 was farming in Britainville with his wife, Sarah, and their four children. In 1885 the hamlet reached its population peak of about ninety. The Britainville church (on the south side of the Highway 542 curve) has recently been restored by the Owen family, who have opened it to the public and are happy to share its history. The church was built in 1877 by James Fisher as a wagon shop. James later operated a harness shop in Gore Bay. The building was originally located across the road, but was moved in 1893 when the present church site was donated. It began a new life as the Behulah Methodist Church. It closed as the United Church in 1969, though it was used sporadically thereafter by the community.

Approximately 6 km (3.5 miles) farther east is Spring Bay. The community was originally known as Cavemount. Its post office was officially established in 1897. It was relocated in 1914 from a more remote waterfront site after its mill closed. The new site was probably chosen for being on the highway and more centrally located for the farming community. From Spring Bay you may drive about 5 km (3 miles) north to the hamlet of Perivale, on Lake Kagawong. This is a worthwhile trip for anyone interested in local art and antiques, as it is the home of the Perivale Gallery. Along with antiques and handicrafts you will find works by such internationally acclaimed island artists as Jack Whyte and Ivan Wheale.

South on the Lake Huron shore is the former hamlet of Lonely Bay, now a cottage area. The community was founded when the Evans and Phillips families established shingle and saw mills in the fall of 1880. According to the 1881 census, Frank Evans was a lumberman from Prince Edward Island and Alfred, Abraham, and Peter Phillips, Ontarians of German descent, were carpenters. Between Lonely Bay and Spring Bay lies Grimsthorpe, named for Samuel Grimes, its first postmaster in 1889. Samuel lived here with his wife, Annie, until they moved to western Canada.

About 2 km (1.2 miles) east of Spring Bay is the Salem Missionary Church. Its founder, William Schroeder, visited the area in 1885, and settled in 1888. George Hartley deeded the site to the Mennonite Church in 1891 and the building was constructed the same year. George, his wife, Frances, and their five children farmed here; their descendants still farm here. The church was founded as the Mennonite Brethren in Christ Church. It became the United Missionary Church in 1949 when members no longer considered themselves 'strict Mennonite,' and in 1969 joined with a United States congregation to become the Salem Missionary Church. Ted Legg, a local farmer, may brief you on the history of his church and community. The Mennonite Legg family was established by 1881, headed by English farmer William Legg. Between 1881 and 1891 this township grew from one Mennonite family to about one dozen. Island settlers' religions were as varied as their origins. According to the 1891 census, the religious affiliations in Campbell Township included Presbyterian, Church of England, Baptist, Mennonite, Plymeth Brethren, Salvation Army, Free Thinker, Christian, Church of Disciples, and Christian Brethren. About 2 km (1.2 miles) farther, at the south turn, is the former district school. From the school corner you head south through Dryden's Corner to Providence Bay, a spot well worth a visit, especially to relax on the island's most beautiful beach.

Before heading to Providence Bay, however, you may wish to detour about 8 km (5 miles) northeast to the Mindemoya Lake Cave. If so, turn east on Highway 542 at Dryden's Corner (marked by the Hawberry House gift shop and Bud the Spud chip stand) instead of continuing south to Providence Bay. This ancient cave, part of the Rock Garden Terrace Resort, is located high on the bluff above Mindemoya Lake. The detour is covered in more detail in the Mindemoya Lake chapter.

Highway 551, which intersects Highway 542 at Dryden's Corner, leads right through Providence Bay to the beach. There are shops and restaurants here as well as a good hardware store. Providence Bay has more intact shingled buildings than any other island community. They are not only durable, but picturesque. Heading south into town you pass the fairground, site of the Providence Bay annual fair. Established in 1884 by residents Mutchmor and Ogle, the fair is held annually in late summer. It features crafts, horse and livestock judging, games, and sports. This community also hosts an annual Perch Derby and cookout. South of the fairground is the stone United Church, which was built in 1921.

Providence Bay has a long history of settlement. Archaeological evidence unearthed by Thor Conway suggests that hundreds of Odawa natives lived here from about 1600 to 1620. Animal bones, arrowheads, tools, seeds, berries, and fish bones have been unearthed at Providence Bay, indicating a large fishing community. The Odawa were a branch of the Algonquin family, which historically occupied the land from Lake Superior to the Ottawa Valley and east through New England and the Atlantic provinces. Most Odawa lived by fishing and hunting, and practised little agriculture. The site, discovered in 1988, is located on the property of the Providence Bay Tent and Trailer Park, beside the Mindemoya River. The name Providence Bay was first used by Captain Henry Bayfield, who charted the waters between 1817 and 1822. The native name was Kchiaazhwiyiing (sand beach) or Mindimoiesibing, from Mindemoya (Old Woman River).

More recently, Providence Bay was a small native camp in the 1840s. Although isolated, it was on a good water route, via the Mindemoya River and Mindemoya Lake to West Bay, and was next to fishing and sugarbush land. The camp of about eighteen people moved to the West Bay reserve in 1872 as a result of the 1862 treaty.

Providence Bay also has a history of timbering colonization. In November 1870 investors Thomas Garland, Ralph W. Mutchmor, and John R. McNiven of Caledonia, Ontario, formed the Providence Bay Milling Company. In return for the mill privileges on the Mindemoya River at Providence Bay and land patents the investors were to purchase their lots for cash, put a settler on each of the lots, and build a grist mill along with their saw mill. The terms of the agreement were completed and a small settlement grew around the mills. The first dock was built in 1872 out of mill slabs. The Providence Bay post office was established in 1874 with John W. Mutchmor as the first postmaster. Ralph W. Mutchmor, born around 1829, was sole owner of the Providence Bay Milling Company by 1881 and his sons John

W. and Benjamin assisted in the business. The town was surveyed in 1879, but the *Manitoulin Expositor* predicted that the one-fifth–acre town lots were not likely to be snapped up at the rather steep price of $50 each. By October the newspaper proclaimed that the village was at last making a start, with several buildings completed or in progress. The new year saw two young merchants, Samuel Wabb and John Johnson, open a store, Robert Foster build a hotel, and John Walden start a boarding house. By spring, Horace Besant had rented the company's grist mill, and construction of the Presbyterian Church was started. The church was completed in 1880 by Robert W. Fawcett for $645. In 1885 an Episcopal church was erected by James Kendrick.

In 1880 the island was producing and shipping great quantities of railroad ties and pavement posts, providing winter employment for many settlers. Most ties and posts were shipped to the Owen Sound company of James Sutherland. Providence Bay merchants Wabb and Johnson sold thirty-five thousand ties and posts that year. In 1885, according to local papers, the village contained twenty houses, Tinkis's large general store, William Pattison's hotel, Mutchmor's saw and grist mill, a blacksmith shop, and a shoe shop, and was actively shipping lumber, ties, posts, grain, and produce. The community prospered during the 1880s, shipping farm, forest, and fish products, but during the next decade Sutherland's company declined along with the settlement as the forests were depleted.

Two legends are unique to the area. One is the Burning Boat, a phenomenon which occurs during a full moon at about 3 a.m., just offshore from the former site of the lighthouse. It is described as a red burning mass, often with the outline of a sailing ship. It has been seen by as many as thirty to forty people at one time. Sceptics explain it as resulting from hot gases and reflections.

The second legend is the Sailor's Grave. A native walking on the beach was said to have found several sailor's bodies washed ashore. Since he was unfamiliar with white men, he carefully dug graves for them so as not to anger the spirits. The graves were marked by three huge boulders which remain today not far from the beach, between the village and the dock.

Providence Bay is considered by some to be northern Ontario's most attractive beach. It stretches to the horizon and slopes gently into the bay. There is also a playground, picnic area, and washrooms. Next to the beach is the Harbour Centre building, opened in 1990. The building is faced with local limestone containing numerous fossils, and houses a local history and fisheries interpretive centre and a small restaurant featuring Manitoulin's own Farquhar's ice cream. Next to the public beach is a large campground. The Mindemoya River drains into the bay just east of the Harbour Centre. It is one of four major salmon spawning rivers on Manitoulin. The others are the Kagawong River, Blue Jay Creek, and the Manitou River.

The Huron Sands gift shop produces high-quality island-made jam, jelly, honey, chutney, relish, and mustard for sale. North of the Huron Sands stands the tiny St Peter's Anglican chapel. It was built in 1935 on land donated by the Sylvester Berry family. A ship's bell hangs in the belfry. Just east of the Huron Sands an old schoolhouse now houses a restaurant. In the summer a local farmer's market usually takes place on Friday mornings in downtown Providence Bay.

From the town continue southeast along the beach road, past the trailer park, then head east to Michael's Bay and South Baymouth. The first 5 km (3 miles) of the road runs due east through bush and grazing lands, past snake fences, then southeast past a stone and a log farmhouse. Just past the log house is a private road to Carter Bay, an isolated beach backed by sand dunes. Unfortunately, the bay's popularity has seriously damaged its dunes in recent years. Although the area remains one of the best dune systems on the Upper Great Lakes, its future remains uncertain after more than two decades of discussion about development. The beach is accessible by a narrow, rough, winding gravel road about 5 km (3 miles) long, followed by a 15-minute trek over the dunes. Please respect the natural beauty of the site, remove litter, and remain on the trails, remembering this is private property.

The next clearing (1 km past Carter Bay road) is another hiking trail, the Carnarvon–Tehkummah Line. A small parking lot and a sign mark the trail, which heads due south and can be followed as far as Michael's Bay. It follows typical south-shore

Providence Bay, Northern Ontario's most beautiful beach

lowlands of spruce and balsam. The trail is not difficult (a 12 km or 7 mile round trip), although it can be very hot and dry in July, or other times wet owing to its lowland location. It's prudent to take along a pack sack with beverages and snacks.

A further 2.5 km (1.5 miles) leads to Michael's Bay, where you can glimpse the island's south shore in all its rugged, majestic beauty. The solid gravel road continues for about 5 km (3 miles) to the municipal picnic area and boat launch on the shore of the Manitou River. This is the former site of the Michael's Bay settlement, which has now entirely disappeared.

Michael's Bay, like Providence Bay, is the site of an ancient native settlement dating from the 1600s. According to Peter Stork and Thor Conway, the sheltered harbour and adjacent Manitou River and Blue Jay Creek made this an ideal Odawa fishing settlement. In recent history this settlement was unique,

The Carter Bay dunes

Snake fences and former homesteads are scattered along this route.

as it was the only island town whose entire existence was devoted to timbering; appropriately, it was dubbed 'Stumptown.' Its total reliance on timbering accounted for its dramatic rise and decline. In 1866 some Toronto entrepreneurs, Robert A. Lyon and Associates, received a licence to timber 22 square miles in Tehkummah Township, as well as the mill privileges on the Manitou River at Michael's Bay. The island's first timber licence was somewhat controversial, as it was obtained before land and timber licences were sold by public auction, and apparently entailed political intervention. Lyon's partners included his brother William D. Lyon of Milton, Ontario, who spent two years at Michael's Bay establishing the sawmill and mercantile business. By the fall of 1867 the mill was operating and employed twenty men. The firm cut and shipped more than two million feet of pine lumber in 1868 and 1869, and a large number of squared timbers and lath. By 1869 there were, in addition to labourers and lumbermen, about sixty residents, including fishermen, a millwright, a carpenter, a lighthouse keeper, three coopers, and a blacksmith. In 1870 Michael's Bay lighthouse was constructed and lit. It was the second lighthouse station on the island; the first station was composed of two range lights at Little Current, erected in 1866. The cost of the Michael's Bay lighthouse was shared by the federal Department of Marine and Fisheries and the timber company. By the early 1870s the timber limit had increased from 22 to 120 square miles. In the mid-1870s the firm again attempted to increase its holdings, claiming it was short of timber, but the increase was denied. In 1878 the firm, overcome by debt, was forced to assign its timber licence to the Toronto Lumber Company.

Robert A. Lyon was born in Scotland around 1830, and had settled on the island with his wife and four children to run his timber operations. He was elected member of the provincial parliament for the new riding of Algoma in 1878. He was an unusual character, and his exploits as member of the provincial parliament made the local paper. He was famous for travelling by snowshoe from his Manitoulin residence to the legislature in Toronto and accounts of his seasonal trips were published, outlining his timing, mileage, and adventures. The 1 May 1880 edition of the *Manitoulin Expositor* announced that he had left Toronto March 6 and arrived two weeks later on Manitoulin. It proclaimed that he had earned his allowance as he had to tramp on snowshoes 150 to 200 miles each session. In 1890 Lyon received the appointment of the registrarship of East Algoma, located at Sault Ste Marie.

The Michael's Bay town plot was laid out in the summer of 1879. The *Expositor* claimed the shingle and saw mills working full-tilt were producing 3,500 feet of wood and 20,000 shingles daily. It also boasted that the 23-mile-long road from here to Manitowaning was in 'not bad' condition and could be travelled in three-and-one-half hours. By the mid-1880s this was a very active lumber port, with a population of about four hundred, stores, boarding houses, a hotel, taverns, a bakery, a blacksmith shop, a school, and about fifteen frame houses in the town plot and the only lighthouse along the south shore. In September 1882 the Toronto Lumber Company sold out, and R.A. Lyon became manager of the Michael's Bay Timber Company, incorporated in 1882 and licensed to timber 37.9 square miles. But by October 1888 the company was bankrupt. Over the next two decades two serious fires destroyed most of the village.

In 1994, it was accounced that the Blue Jay Creek Provincial Park, a natural environment park, would be created on lands donated by Howard Hindman and the Hindman Timber Company. The park features a ridge and slough landscape of cedar, spruce, and pine forest; the waterfalls which powered the Manitou River's saw and shingle mill; the Manitou River and Blue Jay Creek's spring spawning ground for rainbow trout, and the fall migration route for the trout and pink and chinook salmon; and one of the island's largest wintering grounds for deer, in the shore's dense cedar forest. In addition, the Ministry of Natural Resources has identified as an 'Area of Natural and Scientific Interest' the point where the Manitou River has cut its channel into the edge of a remnant of a raised delta deposited between two limestone ridges centuries ago. The raised delta is the only one noted by the ministry on the island. Raised beaches mark the position of former ancient shorelines, and the area also possesses the best ridge and swale system on Manitoulin. According to Stewart Hilts, in John B. Theberge's *Legacy: The Natural History of Ontario*, one of the most spectacular series of former storm beach ridges in Ontario south of Hudson Bay extends inland from Michael's Bay, where a prehistoric narrow bay was gradually filled in by sandbars. About 7 km (4 miles) from this site are 'cabbage heads,' crystallized spheroids measuring up to 30 cm in diameter, the fossilized remains of plants which existed here many thousands of years ago when the island was covered by warm seas.

If you have been touring at length on Manitoulin you may have noticed the abundance of deer. In 1990 the deer population was especially high and was estimated at 20,000. The annual November deer hunt attracts about 6,000 hunters who retrieve several thousand deer. Manitoulin participates in the successful Hats for Hides program in which hunters exchange deer hides for collectible hats. The hides are then sold at reasonable prices to aboriginal artists. In 1880, caribou, not deer, populated Manitoulin; however, within five years large herds of red deer appeared at Michael and Providence bays.

From Michael's Bay continue east into Tehkummah. You will travel through pretty rolling farmland with a number of unique outbuildings. Tehkummah is described in the Manitou Lake tour. Just east of Tehkummah, Highway 6 leads south to South Baymouth or north into Manitowaning and Little Current.

TEN

The Eastern Bays
(Tour 3)

South Baymouth to Little Current,
from the island's southeastern ferry port
to the northeastern tip and bridge

The eastern tour is 63 km (about 38 miles) long. Allow half a day to enjoy this route, or longer if you wish to explore the east coast's century-old farmsteads, museums, waterfalls, native territory, and lighthouses.

The tour begins at South Baymouth, or Zaagdawaang, meaning 'the outlet,' as it was known by the original inhabitants. Located near fishing, sugarbush, and water transportation, it was a natural native camp-site. Between the 1840s and 1860s there was a small settlement on South Bay (fifty-three persons by 1860) who joined the main reserves in the late 1860s. By 1867 only about thirty people lived here: Chief Wabenasemin, Thomas Keeshkakkoo's family, and about twenty-one others.

The only Protestant clergyman, Jabez Waters Sims of Manitowaning, served this remote group (not all of whom were Christians), and recorded in his journal details of their camp. Their wigwams varied in location from year to year: they were in the swamp area in 1867. Thomas Keeshkakkoo appears to have been educated by the missionaries at Manitowaning, as he expressed an interest in reading texts and music books to Sims and his predecessor. On 5 January 1867, Chief Wabenasemin fell on the ice and Rev. Sims travelled by snowshoe for four-and-a-half hours from Manitowaning over deep snow, logs, and rocky ground to attend to the dying man. Sims spent that night with the Keeshkakkoo family in their wigwam. In what would be cramped quarters by modern standards, the approximately 10-foot-square residence accommodated a very extended family: Thomas, his wife, a widow, a cousin, a daughter, and her two little sons. Three days later Sims returned to bury the chief. The chief's funeral, attended by twenty-two natives, was held in his wigwam. After the service, one side of the wigwam was pulled down and the coffin was carried from the swamp to a clearing, where it was put on a sleigh and pulled by eight men to the burial ground, half a mile away. After the graveside service, the coffin was covered with birchbark.

Fishing and transportation have always been the area's main focus. The first non-native settlers here were members of the Perrott family, who settled temporarily in July 1854. American citizens, they came to fish under the new Reciprocity Treaty between Canada and the United States. They soon moved to Wikwemikong, where they remained for six years.

South Baymouth was re-established as a fishing station by the Wilman and Ritchie families around 1878. The Wilmans had been fishing on the island since at least 1871, and had moved here from Walker Point 5 km (3 miles) to the west. South Baymouth had a better natural harbour and was closer to Manitowaning, by water up South Bay. In 1871 the family consisted of Val Wilman Sr, born around 1797 in Canada, his wife, Lovina, granddaughter Lovina and her husband, William Ritchie, and grandson Val, born around 1859. Val Wilman Sr's two sons were said to have drowned while taking a load of fish to market. Wilman's catch was salted and shipped out via Killarney, on the North Shore, to the Buffalo Fish Company. In 1879 the company switched to shipping fresh fish. The Buffalo Fish Company also operated the first store in town. Around 1881 Hiram Tinkis opened a hotel but the fishing industry remained the town's primary raison d'être, and in 1891 the census recorded six fishing families: Green, Chisholm, Sim, Ritchie, Wilman, and Owen.

Fishing is still a popular pastime, both on the inland lakes and rivers as well as on the Manitoulin shores. Salmon is a favourite catch, and thirty-pound fish can be found in the waters of South Bay, Providence Bay, and Meldrum Bay.

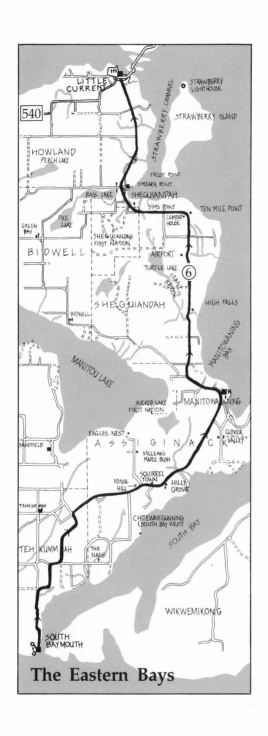

The Eastern Bays

The first public building, a school which also served as the community church, was built in January 1889. The school acquired its belfry and bell in 1938. This typical-looking Manitoulin school was closed in 1962. Today, the Little Red Schoolhouse contains the community's museum. A post office opened in South Baymouth in 1890. Its postmaster, R.P. Green, who held the position for 38 years, was also the proprietor of the first independent store. The first purpose-built church was built around 1891 by the Anglicans and was later replaced by St John's. The Presbyterians also constructed a church, which was replaced in 1927 with today's St Andrew's-by-the-Sea United. As the importance of Michael's Bay declined, South Baymouth became the south shore's main port. In 1898 two square white lighthouses were erected. They were joined in 1929 by a light and bell buoy, presumably to guide the ferry which had been proposed for this location.

Visitors who began their island tour in South Baymouth probably came to Manitoulin Island by ferry. This entrance to the island was inaugurated in 1932 when the Owen Sound Transportation Company was granted the exclusive government franchise to run a ferry between South Baymouth and Tobermory on the Bruce Peninsula to the south. Before this date several vessels provided an irregular ferry service between Tobermory and Providence Bay and South Baymouth. Island ports had been well served by the countless vessels plying Georgian Bay and competing for island business during navigation season since the mid-nineteenth century. The first ferry on the route was the 14-car *Normac*, which made four daily runs. The fare for automobiles was $5 one way or $7 return. Within ten years the *Caribou* was added to the route. In 1947 the new steam-powered 50-car *Norisle* ferry took over the run. The Ontario government placed the ferry service under its Ontario Northland Transportation Commission in the 1960s in an attempt to meet the growing demand for ferry sevice. In 1964 the North Shore route's *Norgoma* joined the *Norisle*. The *Norgoma*, built at Collingwood especially for the Owen Sound to Sault Ste Marie run, was a welcome addition. Its removal from the North Shore route, however, marked the end of an era of service, not just by this vessel but by dozens of previous vessels.

The ferry at South Baymouth

You can visit the *Norisle* at Manitowaning, where it is permanently berthed. The 140-car MS *Chi-Cheemaun* (the Big Canoe)
took over the run in 1974 and was joined in 1989 by the 120-car
MS *Nindawayma* (Little Sister).

Many visitors rush off the ferry to join the long line of cars
travelling north. You should stop and enjoy this village. I highly
recommend the cedar boardwalk adjacent to the marina. The
boardwalk extends over a lagoon, past pitted rock pavement,
and through a gazebo and lookout. This is an ideal retreat for
one to observe and photograph the ferry's arrival or departure.
Next to the dock are a number of gift shops. The Huron Motor
Lodge was opened in 1932 by George and Clara Britten to serve
the ferry traffic. A room and three meals were available for $2.50

a day. At the junction of Highway 6 is St Andrew's-by-the-Sea; farther on are the Little Red Schoolhouse museum and St John's Anglican Church. John Budd Memorial Park, a municipal campground named for one of the area's first fishery researchers, is located here, and north of town is the Tehkummah Township public beach, on South Bay. The large land mass across from South Baymouth's ferry landing is the southwestern tip of the Wikwemikong Peninsula, which is described later in this tour.

The former South Baymouth's Ontario Fisheries Research Station is located 4 km (2.4 miles) north on Highway 6. It was closed in 1993 for economic reasons. The Station was established by the Department of Lands and Forests in 1947 to investigate the declining fish populations. Research on fish migration, sport and commercial fishing, and the splake population was carried on here.

You are travelling through Tehkummah Township. Established in 1866, it was named for Louis Tekoma (Tehkummah), originally Tekomassima. Born around 1815 in Harbor Springs, Michigan, he emigrated to Manitoulin in the 1840s, after the 1836 treaty made the entire island a reserve for all natives who were loyal to the British. Louis died at the age of 80 and was buried in the Catholic cemetery in Wikwemikong. Tehkummah was a figure of controversy for a number of years. He was one of only two native Wikwemikong chiefs who signed the 1862 treaty to cede the island. He and Paimsahdung were temporarily expelled from Wikwemikong for signing the treaty, which was strongly opposed by Wikwemikong natives and priests.

At the time of survey and settlement in the 1860s numerous native clearings for gardens, corn, and potato pits were found in Tehkummah Township. The largest was just south of the Slash settlement on South Bay.

A continuation of the Niagara Escarpment, Manitoulin can be described as a huge limestone rock formation which is tilted down towards the southwest where it slides into Lake Huron. You are at present travelling along the highest side of this rock mass.

Just north of the Highway 542 junction is Gordon's Park

where an eighteen-hole miniature golf course, archery range, and a nature trail are popular activities.

This is Assiginack Township, surveyed in 1865 and named after John-Baptiste Assiginack (1768–1866), also known as Siginock, Sakinaugh, l'Etourneau, Blackbird, and Assiginaugh. Like Louis Tehkummah, he migrated from Harbor Springs, Michigan. He arrived via Drummond Island, where he was employed as an interpreter until 1827. He returned to Harbor Springs and moved to Penetanguishene in 1830, Coldwater in 1832, and then to Manitoulin to join the Wikwemikong settlement.

Assiginack is a controversial hero, respected by the government and his own people for somewhat different reasons. Government documents reveal him to be a valuable war ally, an interpreter, a Roman Catholic convert, and a signatory of both the 1836 and 1862 treaties. Though his endorsement and signature on the 1862 treaty turned many in the native community against him, he was still recognized as a great war chief. He is remembered for his many feats at the battles at Michilimackinac and Beaver Dams during the War of 1812, for which he is believed to have received a medal from the British. By 1864 he was a resident of Manitowaning, where the Wikwemikong priests visited him regularly. Assiginack's son Francis was selected by the Indian Department to attend Upper Canada College in 1842, along with three other native boys. Francis did very well at the school, and was employed by the Indian Department after his graduation until his death in 1863. Another son, Benjamin, married Louis Tehkummah's daughter Mary Ann Samigokwe. Descendants of Chief Assiginack still live on the island.

The landscape changes rapidly here, from rolling farmland to cedar bush. Notice the traditional snake fences; both portable and practical, they are easily erected by farmers using Manitoulin's abundant cedar.

To hike through a beautiful maple bush turn left on the New England Road (also called Eagle's Nest). McLean Park is 3 km (2 miles) north, on the right side of the intersection of New England and McLean roads. This beautiful park, about 40 ha (100 acres), was donated in 1989 by Donald E. McLean in memory of his parents Donald McLean (1863–1951) and Sarah McKechnie McLean (1872–1938). Donald E. McLean inherited the property in 1937 and lived there until 1987. Mr McLean tapped the trees for syrup, but did not harvest the wood. In his 88th year he decided to share the property with the public in perpetuity. The island was once dotted with numerous sugar bush lots. By the 1850s traders were visiting Manitoulin to exchange wares for maple sugar and fish. Island natives sold 116,716 pounds of maple sugar in 1857 alone. In 1858 the resident Anglican missionary, Peter Jacobs, described the sugaring activity at Manitowaning: 'Some of the sugar camps are 3 miles away, they remain in the bush as long as the sap runs, each family makes 10–15 barks or mokauks of sugar, each weighing 70 pounds, sold at about 4 pence sterling a pound.' Non-native settlers also learned how to tap the trees to collect sap. Robert Tustian, son of Billings Township pioneers, remembered their native neighbours' providing his parents with wooden spikes and birchbark troughs for tapping and collecting the sap.

East of the highway is the Slash settlement, named for a pioneer firebreak, and located on the Murray River, which supplied power for a sawmill. The Slash Anglican Church was opened in 1900 on land donated by pioneer William McMurray. The post office opened in 1889. Tehkummah School Section Four school was built here in 1883.

Opposite the Slash Road is a wood frame farmhouse and the remains of an island barn. Just past the Slash Road, at the junction of the highway and New England Road, is Fossil Hill, where fossils can be seen in the rock on both sides of the highway. Enjoy exploring this unique area, but please leave the fossils for others to enjoy.

Directly south, on South Bay, is the former native camp of South Bay West or Chitewaiegunning. It was established in the 1840s, and by 1850 had a population of twenty-five Catholics and twenty-five Anglicans. In 1870 the group's request that their land be set aside as a reserve was denied. The band then moved to the Wikwemikong Peninsula where they formally amalgamated with the Wikwemikong natives in 1968.

On the east side of the highway, just past Fossil Hill in the Squirrel Town settlement, is the homestead of William Sproat. In October 1870 William's wife Mary died here, leaving William to raise their seven children, aged 3 to 18 years. He remarried and

McLean Park

raised six more children. In June 1879, according to the *Manitoulin Expositor*, William disturbed a native grave while ploughing his field. He found two skeletons: a man wearing beaded leggings, a waist sash, and bearing a tin pail, and a woman with a hatchet. They were immediately reburied in the field.

The short road on the right just past Fossil Hill and Sproat's homestead leads to the Sim settlement. Robert Sim, who was born in 1828 in Arbroath, Scotland, his wife, Isabella, and their family settled here in 1869. Travelling from Mono Township, Ontario, they came to Manitoulin by boat via South Bay and established themselves as farmers and fishermen.

The Hilly Grove church and cemetery is next, on the east side. The white frame Hilly Grove Pioneer Chapel was built in 1903. The oldest headstone dates from 1879 and belongs to Ann Ingram. Also buried here are pioneers such as John Rutledge, who had settled here in 1871. John, who was born in Canada of Irish parents, was the first postmaster in 1876. He donated the land for the cemetery and church.

Hilly Grove was Assiginack Township's second post office. By the 1880s the mail was arriving by stagecoach, twice weekly in summer and weekly in winter. The mail route originated in Manitowaning and continued to Tehkummah, Michael's Bay, and Providence Bay. According to an 1884–5 directory of Ontario, Hilly Grove had a population of fifteen and a school. The highway to Manitowaning was built in the early 1870s by the lumber company owned by R.A. Lyon of Michael's Bay. Hilly Grove is a beautiful settlement with picturesque wood, shingle, and log farmsteads surrounded by cedar bush.

Just before the greenhouses of Rainbow Gardens stands an original frame farmhouse which features a centre gable over the front door and original island wood siding. This stands on land sold to Donald McDougall in 1871. By 1901, McDougall's neighbour's son William Haner, a 32-year-old farmer of Irish descent, lived here with his wife and three young children. Prior to 1871, the land between Squirrel Town and Black Rock Roads, along the shore of South Bay, was the South Bay West settlement. The resident natives, pressured by both the 1862 treaty's terms and the encroaching white settlements, were paid for their improvements to the land and were relocated to new island reserves.

Along this road are many examples of the typical Manitoulin farmhouses described in chapter 5.

In 1879 the area was named Clover Valley. Rainbow Gardens, the local plant nursery, continues the island's 125-year gardening tradition. The first recorded amateur horticulturist is the Rev. Jabez Waters Sims, who was Anglican missionary to the native residents from 1864 to 1869. As well as ministering to their spiritual needs, he attempted to arouse the natives' interest in agriculture to help them become more independent as government support waned and new settlers arrived. Sims arrived in October 1864, and following a long cruel winter of subsistence living he planted a substantial garden for his own and his native neighbours' use. He planted seeds carefully transported from Dungannon, Huron County, Ontario, the results of several years' exchange with his parishioners there. The garden produced a surprising variety of plants: melons, cucumber, early kent peas, long pole beans, spinach, lettuce, sage, little silver skin onions, bush beans, peppergrass, cauliflower, tomatoes, celery, parsley, bunch peas, windsor beans, potatoes, onions, radishes, Dr Layton's lettuce (named for the island surgeon), horehound, carrots, parsnips, and Mr Young's peas.

To visit the Wikwemikong Peninsula, turn right from Highway 6 and follow the road southeast around Manitowaning Bay. The eighteen-hole M'nidoo Valley Golf Course is located here. This large peninsula must be toured by car, though there are many opportunities to explore areas on foot. A good place to start is the village of Wikwemikong, via Two O'Clock and Buzwah.

The Two O'Clock settlement, where the road leaves the shore and moves inland, is marked by a few houses located on or near Stephens Cove on Manitowaning Bay. The white frame St Romuald's Church, renamed and rededicated as Gchitwaa Niyaans (Saint Ignatius) in 1992, serves the village of Buzwah and adjacent Mocassets Landing. The area is named for residents Jean-Baptiste Bezwah Sr and Joseph Mocosik, both born in the United States around 1815 and living here with their families by 1871. The road in front of the church leads to a brief but scenic detour to the bay. The studio of local artist James Simon Mishibinijima is located here on the bay. In 1991 Simon's painting *Togetherness*, symbolizing international unity and harmony, was accepted by the Vatican for its collection.

According to Father J. Edward O'Flaherty, Wikwemikong in Ojibwe means 'at the gravel bottom bay' (others translate it as 'bay of the beaver'). This 12,140 ha (30,000 acre) peninsula in Georgian Bay boasts the island's longest history of continuous settlement. Beginning around 1833 natives settled here from Harbor Croche, Michigan; Coldwater, Ontario; and various points in Quebec. The first settlers were the families of Wakegi-ijik, Kinochemeg, Michael Gimoshkam, and Vincent Adawish. When Rev. Adam Elliott and Thomas G. Anderson of the Indian Department visited in 1835 they found five or six Catholic Odawa families, formerly from Lake Michigan. In 1836 Father Jean-Baptiste Proulx (1808–81), a diocesan priest from Penetan-guishene, settled here. When writer Anna Jameson attended the annual gift-giving ceremony in 1837 at Manitowaning she spoke to Father Crue (Proulx). He informed her he had been there two years with a band of Odawas; the settlement had large planta-tions of corn and potatoes, log huts, a chapel, and a priest's house.

By 1842 Wikwemikong village contained 78 buildings for 94 families, including 73 native houses, houses for the school-teacher and priests, a church, a school, and a sawmill. In 1844 the Jesuits took over this mission. This religious order, which first came to Canada with Champlain about two hundred years earlier, was expelled from the country when the Britain defeated France, but returned in 1837. Father Jean-Pierre Choné from Sarnia and his interpreter Ferdinand Roque joined the Wik-wemikong settlement in 1844, and the following year Father Joseph Hannipeaux arrived. By 1846 the area had grown to 502 residents, and by 1858 to almost 600. By that time there were 580 Roman Catholic residents, two priests (Reverends Joseph Hannipeaux and Martin Ferard), a stone church, a mission house, 139 houses, barns, stables, outhouses, and two schools for the 125 schoolchildren.

Under the Jesuits, the Wikwemikong settlement prospered and new smaller villages such as Wikwemikongsing, Chitewaie-gunning, and Buzwah were established. In contrast, the federal government's native settlement experiment at Manitowaning

Wikwemikong Health Centre

across the bay was floundering. The government believed the solution to its lack of success lay in placing native residents on reserved land and opening the entire island for white settlement. The Wikwemikong natives successfully opposed the settlement negotiations and the subsequent treaty of 1862. As a result, the peninsula was not ceded to the government with the rest of Manitoulin.

After successfully resisting the treaty in 1862, Wikwemikong encountered a new pressure: oil exploration. Residents faced the prospect with mixed feelings. In 1864 two oil speculators, W.L. Baby of Windsor and J.R. Berthelott of Milwaukee, sought a licence to drill near Wikwemikong village. The licence was granted and drilling began in 1865. Initial results were promising. By 1867, however, great expense had produced minimal results and this and other oil speculation ceased. Oil speculation was revived several times over the next century, but with meagre results.

Continuing north to Wikwemikong you drive by the commu-

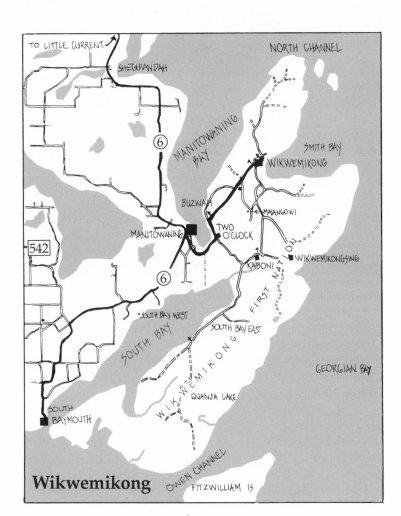

nity cemetery, about 2 km (1.2 miles) past Buzwah, and two whitewashed log cabins 2 km (1.2 miles) farther, next to the war memorial. This memorial, a cross on a cobblestone base, was built by local stonemason Dominic Odjig.

In the village of Wikwemikong, a complex of new buildings stands on the right. On the immediate right is the Wikwemikong Health Centre. This unique facility opened in 1988, and features modern medicine combined with traditional native medicine, including a sweat lodge. The plan of the building is in the shape of an eagle. The entrance is highlighted by poles which, as in traditional wigwam construction, hold symbolic values. Next to the Health Centre are the band's administrative offices, Education Department, and the Tribal Police. The Rainbow Lodge Recovery Centre is situated behind the Health Centre. Next is the Hub Centre daycare and nursery school, which opened in 1990. The log building is Amik-ook Gahmic, or the Elders' Centre. It was built by the Wikwemikong Log Construction Company in 1984.

Drive along Wikwemikong Way to Holy Cross Mission Church. The village has a wide variety of residences, from modern bungalows to traditional whitewashed log cabins. The church, a handsome stone building, was constructed entirely by the native community more than 140 years ago. In 1848, the resident Jesuit priests and parishioners began planning a permanent church. Father Nicholas Point, the Holy Cross Mission's second Jesuit Superior and an experienced artist and architect, is credited with the church's design. Construction began in June 1849 using local materials and labour. The cornerstone was laid on the day of the feast of St Ignatius, 31 July 1849. At that time most of the 3-foot-thick foundation wall had been completed. The church opened in 1852. The interior was gutted by fire in 1954. The building was rebuilt using the original stone walls. Note the doors, designed and built by local artisans Randy Trudeau, Gary Manitowabi, and Eleanor Kanasawe. A large stylized cross is surrounded by the circle of life highlighted by four colours representing the world's four races.

The ruins next to the church were also created by the 1954 fire. The ruins commemorate over one-and-a-half centuries of education here. Wikwemikong has had a school since at least

A square-log whitewashed cabin overlooks the bay.

1842, when Charles La Morandiere, the son of a Shebahaning (Killarney) trader, taught here. By 1857 there were 125 children in the school learning knitting, carding, spinning, weaving, embroidery, fishing, and farming. In the 1880s large frame schools were built. They were later destroyed by fire and rebuilt in stone. In 1913 the non-local children were moved to a new school at Spanish after fire again destroyed the girls' school. Wikwemikong's remaining school served as a day school until it burned, along with the church, in 1954. Schools for native children were also established at Manitowaning (1838), Little Current (1863), Sheguiandah (1867), Shesheguaning (1869), and Sucker Creek and West Bay (1870). Across the street is Jennesseaux Hall, which was built in 1860. Underneath the modern siding stands the original log building, which was used as a church while Holy Cross was being rebuilt. The hall is named for Brother Jennesseaux, who arrived here in 1852. Born in Reims, France, he died in 1884 at the age of 75. Just north of the church a new rectory was built in 1990–1. Pause here to enjoy the view of Smith Bay, which some people believe is the actual site of the 1648 Jesuit mission, rather than at Ten Mile Point (a site farther north on this tour).

The cemetery is home to the Wikwemikong War Memorial, unveiled on Remembrance Day in 1992. The peaceful area contains stones commemorating some of the village's first residents, including Chief Louis Wakegijig, who died in 1899 at the age of 89.

Wikwemikong is the origin of most of the tipi structures seen on Manitoulin. Stanley T. Peltier, an Odawa, re-creates tipis in the traditional Plains manner, using hand-peeled cedar or balsam poles. White canvas is used in place of the traditional covering of skins. Construction follows time-honoured methods and symbolism. The fourteen inside poles are all named and numbered; for example, pole number 7 represents kinship, pole number 14, ultimate protection. The entrance is always set to the east, to the rising sun. Construction begins with a basic tripod, tied with a rope 14 m (45 feet) long wrapped clockwise (the direction of the sun's travel). The remaining poles are tied on, and the canvas is attached. Historically, tipis were built by Plains natives, and are not indigenous to the island. Manitoulin and other eastern natives constructed wigwams, which were similar in structure but covered in bark.

In 1995 a new Wikwemikong marina was opened. The large log building houses an interpretive centre, gift shop, marine facilities, and dining-room.

You may wish to continue north to see the upper portion of this peninsula. Unfortunately, you will require an all-terrain vehicle to tour the northernmost reaches.

Cultural activities flourish here and many outstanding artists and craftspeople are active in 'Wiky.' Wikwemikong is famous for its powwow, held annually since 1960 on the Civic Holiday weekend in August. Native dancers and musicians from across North America attend and compete for prizes. The colourful costumes are breathtaking, the dancing spectacular. The intertribal dances, when everyone from preschoolers to elders participates, are particularly enjoyable. The hoop, jingle, and rabbit dances are fascinating. The drums are the heartbeat of the festiv-

ities. The lead dancers, one man and one woman who participate in all the dances, encourage young dancers and serve as
models. An annual local art exhibition is held in the school
during the powwow. It is well worth visiting to see the latest
works of nationally recognized artists and discover emerging
new talent.

One of Canada's two native professional theatres is located
on the Wikwemikong Peninsula. The De-ba-jeh-mu-jig (storyteller) Theatre performs here each summer and tours through
the remainder of the year. In 1990 their presentation of *Toronto at
Dreamer's Rock* gained the troupe national acclaim.

Across the street from the powwow grounds is the Odjig residence. Built of logs in 1882 by Jonas Odjig, the unique home was
remodelled by his stonemason son Dominic using stone, logs,
and concrete. Note the decorative fence, and flower bed.

For an alternative route off the peninsula, follow the road
from town which runs along the south shore of Smith Bay, then
heads south. About 5 km (3 miles) south is the Maiangowi settlement, presumably named for Louis Maiangowi, who was
born about 1819 in the United States and was farming here with
his family by 1871.

The southerly road ends at Kaboni. Turn right for Manitowaning or points farther south. Kaboni features a Catholic
church, a small one-room school, a firehall, and residences.
About 2.5 km (1.5 miles) east of Kaboni is Wikwemikongsing, a
small hamlet which has existed since 1846, when it had a population of fifty-two. At the next intersection turn right to return to
Manitowaning, or continue straight through to the village of
South Bay East, on South Bay. On the shore here is Our Lady of
Grace Church. The land south of this point remains largely inac-
cessible. In the centre of the territory, 5 km (3 miles) south of
South Bay East, is Quanja Lake. Wilderness camps have been
held here since 1989 in an effort to preserve Anishnaabe (native)
culture. Survival skills, swimming, canoeing, and fishing are
offered. From South Bay East, return to the last intersection and
turn left, to Manitowaning.

The Wikwemikong Peninsula is separated from the rest of
the island by two bays, South Bay and Manitowaning Bay. In
the 1820s Captain Henry Bayfield, who surveyed the area,

Wikwemikong powwow dancers

named Manitowaning Bay the Heywood Sound, and South Bay the Manitoulin Gulf. Both bodies of water were renamed in the 1860s. Manitowaning received the Ojibwe name for 'den of the Great Spirit.' The bays are separated by a 3 km (2 mile) neck of land containing, according to native legend, a secret underwater passage which the Kitche Manitou (Great Spirit) uses to travel between the bays.

From Wikwemikong, along the bay, turn north into the village of Manitowaning. Parking is available on Arthur Street, between the museum and downtown, just a few blocks north. This is a pretty town to explore on foot. Highlights include the museum, the roller mills, the old *Norisle* ferry, downtown, the lighthouse, and St Paul's Church.

The village of Manitowaning arose as a result of the 1836 treaty. It was to be the centre of government Indian administration and of the Anglican mission for the island. In October 1838 Manitowaning was settled by a government party consisting of thirty-four persons, including Captain Anderson of the Indian Department, an Anglican clergyman, a doctor, a teacher, their families, as well as oarsmen and mechanics. By 1842 Manitowaning contained three workshops, a store, barn, schoolhouse, sawmill, eleven houses for employees, and thirty-seven native houses. The government intended to teach the natives trades and agriculture and educate their children, but the settlement grew slowly and attempts to 'Europeanize' the natives were mostly unsuccessful. The local superintendent, Charles Dupont, attributed the lack of success mainly to the absence of fishing in both summer and winter. The closest fishing ground was four miles west at Manitou Lake. By 1858 many Manitowaning natives had left. Only twenty-two houses remained, with no regular school, workshops, or field work. The Rev. Peter Jacobs, a native from the Red River area of Manitoba and one of two resident Anglican clergymen here at the time, remarked sadly on this period: 'last month [written 27 March 1858] James Wahbegagkake, one of our chiefs died (White Hawk) about 55 years old, he was the father of a young woman who died last summer, and a son one fortnight later. He leaves a widow and 2 children, of the 12 he has had, only 2 are left. There are many other Indians here, who once had many children of whom very few are now living. It makes one sad sometimes to think how fast the Indians are disappearing in this as well as other parts of Canada. Like the snow in spring are they melting away.'

The Manitowaning experiment failed. Wikwemikong, however, flourished, and although a recommendation was made that the island continue as a haven for wandering bands, settlement pressure led to a second treaty in 1862. The treaty assigned certain reserves to the native population; the remainder of the island, with the exception of the Wikwemikong Peninsula, was sold to non-native settlers.

In 1864 High Chief John Mizhequongi lived here with eleven families (fifty-six people). Mizhequongi was born around 1806 in Upper Canada. The 1861 Ontario census showed three chiefs in Manitowaning, the other two being Assiginack and Tehkummah (mentioned earlier in this tour). Most of the government's financial support had been withdrawn from the settlement by 1864. Only the natives and an Anglican clergyman, a government superintendent, a clerk, and a doctor remained. Around 1867 the Manitowaning natives, pressured by the terms of the 1862 treaty, accompanied their clergyman to the newly created Sheguiandah reserve. With this move, Manitowaning became almost a ghost town, leaving only the three government employees. Since the superintendent was also the land agent, all settlers eventually passed through and Manitowaning quickly became populated by non-native entrepreneurs.

The Manitowaning town plot was surveyed in 1873, and the first lot was sold in July 1875. By February 1880, according to the *Manitoulin Expositor* (established in Manitowaning in 1879), the town contained three churches, the land office, a government wharf, two licensed hotels (the Commercial and Queens), five general stores, a drug store, a resident doctor, two harness makers, two cabinetmakers, a tailor, two bootmakers, three blacksmiths, a butcher, a baker, a printing office, a watchmaker, two steam planing mills, Campbell's steam grist and woolen mill, an agricultural hall, and residences. Fifty-three buildings had been constructed or enlarged since the previous summer. This was Manitowaning's most prosperous era. It was considered the focus of the new tourism industry by the local newspa-

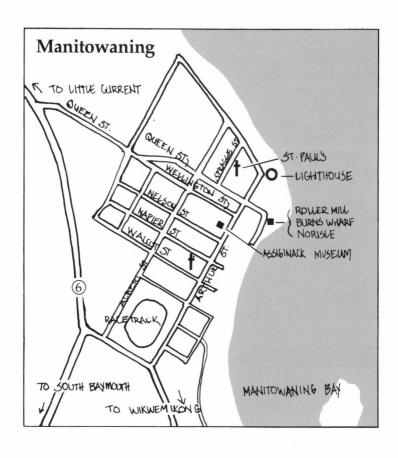

per. Unfortunately, its growth was hampered by not being on the main steamer routes.

W.L. Smith founded the *Manitoulin Expositor* in a building downtown between Tinkis's store and the Commercial Hotel. Ten years later, as the town and the island boomed, he recalled his trip from Barrie, Ontario, in March 1879 over ice and snow. At nightfall, his native guides dug out snow-beds and lined them with spruce branches. More evergreens were placed on the windward side of the hole and a fire was started at the foot of the snow bed to keep the group from freezing.

The Presbyterian Church, now a United Church, was established on 15 October 1878. Its contractor was John Purdy of the Manitowaning Planing Mills. Today, like many island churches, it is well-known for its fundraising church suppers attended by residents and visitors. The church is located just southwest of the museum.

The Assiginack Museum, on Arthur Street, was built as a 'lockup' in 1878 by the Ontario Department of Public Works. It was constructed by the Law Building Company of Meaford, Ontario, which also built the Little Current and Gore Bay lockups. Manitowaning and Little Current's lockups were tendered together and built at a total cost of $4,119. Public Works architect Kivas Tully supervised their design and specifications. Tully was also responsible for the Gore Bay court-house design eleven years later. He was one of the most talented architects of his time and his buildings remain some of the island's most impressive landmarks. The lockup's original furnishings included six chairs, a table, a desk with pigeon holes, two wood stoves with pipes, five single iron bedsteads, and five iron buckets, at a total cost of $92. In May 1882 the Meaford Building Company began work on an addition to the lockup. Later the building housed the municipal offices and library before being converted to a museum in 1965. Also on the museum grounds are a blacksmith shop, a barn, a house, and a school.

Manitowaning was home to a number of long-standing businesses. Stella's Shop was opened in 1926 by Stella Sim (Robbins), moving to its Queen Street location in 1931. Niece Phyllis Atkinson continued to run the shop after Stella's death in 1994.

Mastin's store downtown had a long history, from 1879

The Assiginack Museum was built as a 'lockup' in 1878.

through 1990. It was established in 1879 by John Reynolds as a boot and shoemaking business, and operated by his descendants. The original store burned down in 1893 and was immediately rebuilt, reportedly modelled after Chicago's enormous Marshall Fields Store. Constructed of stone in hopes of preventing future fires, it had the latest in modern glass shopfronts. In 1924 John Reynolds died, leaving the store to his only child, 20-year-old Catherine. She capably ran the store for six years. In 1930 Catherine married Arthur Mastin, who took over the store and later changed the name to Mastin's. In 1994 the building was reopened for business.

Another early merchant in Manitowaning was Charles Woodward, who later founded the Woodward's Department Store chain in western Canada. According to *The Woodwards* by Douglas E. Harker, it was on Manitoulin that Charles developed the 'cash only' policy on which he based his retail empire. In 1875 he arrived on the island and purchased 200 acres of land at Manitou Lake in Bidwell Township. When he visited the property he found it too stony for farming so he opened a small trading post there instead. The following year he moved his business to Manitowaning where, although there were four general stores, there was a much larger market. He built a frame store on High Street between Winkler's Hardware and Mitchell's blacksmith shop. He and his partner John Anderson, who was also his brother-in-law, were forced to close in 1879 when they were cheated by a supplier and a customer. In September 1879 an ad in the local paper proclaimed the business would be carried on by Charles Woodward alone and 'the books will be closed against credit' in Woodward's Cash Store. He sold the business to Thomas Parkinson in 1881 and headed west to the Manitoba boom. Defeated by the Manitoba bust, he returned to the island and purchased Thompson's store in Gore Bay in May 1882. In 1885 he bought a second store, in Thessalon on the mainland North Shore. When this business burned down in 1890, after twelve years on Manitoulin, he headed west to Vancouver where he eventually prospered, creating the Woodward's department store empire.

In 1879 John Purdy opened the Manitowaning Planing Mills on the south side of Wellington Street. The *Manitoulin Expositor* of 19 July 1879 announced that the new shingle mill was in operation and that the previous Tuesday, George E. Green had purchased the first lumber ever dressed on Manitoulin. Purdy was born around 1838 in Ireland and arrived on Manitoulin via Owen Sound in the 1870s. The business remained in the Purdy family through three generations, until the 1960s.

The Manitoulin Roller Mills, which began grinding flour in February 1883 as the J.T. Burns steam and flour mill, still stands on the waterfront. In studying the mill for the Historic Sites and Monuments Board of Canada, C.J. Taylor noted the Burns mill used the 'new process' of gradual reduction by millstones rather than the old process of fast reduction. The gradual process allowed Manitoulin's main crop, spring wheat, to yield a higher quality and quantity of whiter, livelier flour. The first grist and flour mill on the island had been built in Sheguiandah in 1871. Alex Campbell built Manitowaning's first and the island's fifth grist and flour mill in 1878. Unlike the earlier island mill sites, Manitowaning lacked water power and had to use more expensive steam power. The Burns mill was designed by a well-known millwright, E.P. Caves of Thistledown, Ontario. Although plain, the mill was well designed. It consisted of a large rectangular building with a small office extension on the north side, and a stone structure on the east side for the steam engine. The two additions isolated the fire sources of office stove and steam engine from the mill itself. The mill was built on a local rubble stone foundation. Its gambrel roof maximized the attic storage space while the roof's clerestory area provided windows for light and ventilation and held the elevator machinery.

Burns Wharf Theatre, the roller mills, and the former *Norisle* ferry stand on the waterfront.

Rooftop ventilation was very important in preventing spontane-
ous combustion. The fact that the mill is still standing points to
the effectiveness of the design.

In the basement three pairs of large log beams probably supported the mill's grinding wheels. The grain was unloaded and
elevated to the upper floors on the south half of the main floor.
The grinding wheels were probably located behind the loading
area. The north half of the main floor held the mixer. On the second floor, the south end contains a huge storage bin and the
north end has a hopper leading to the mixer below. The top storey has storage bins and supports for the pulley system and the
second elevator. In September 1895 the mill suffered a serious
fire but was immediately restored. The mill was operated by the
Burns family until 1936, when it was sold to William Knechtel
and Son of Hanover, Ontario. It ceased being a grist mill in 1942
when the Edwards Grain Company converted it for seed and
feed supplies. In 1951 the Manitoulin Livestock Cooperative
turned it into a feed mill, for chopping the island's chief crops of
mixed grain, oats, and barley into livestock feed.

The mill now houses agricultural exhibits, and the wharf
warehouse is home to the Burns Wharf Theatre. This local theatre group, in conjunction with the Sudbury Theatre Centre,
produces live summer theatre shows.

Next to the mill is the SS *Norisle*, the last steam-powered passenger ship on the Great Lakes. This 50-car ferry was built in
Collingwood for the trip from Tobermory to South Baymouth,
replacing the 14-car *Normac* and the *Caribou* in 1947. The
Norisle was advertised as 'new, all steel, modern and fireproof.' In 1948 the *Norisle*, made two trips daily and the *Normac* one trip weekly. In 1974 it was replaced by the 140-car
Chi-Cheemaun. Visitors may tour the *Norisle*, a fascinating ship
which is now permanently moored at this site. The SS *Norisle*,
the roller mills, and the nearby Assiginack Museum are all
open daily from June to September. The community hosts the
annual Southeast Manitoulin Lion's Summerfest in July and a
fall fair in early September.

St Paul's Church in Manitowaning is the oldest Anglican parish church in Northern Ontario. It was built between 1845 and
1848 for the island's native community, and has served the area

for 145 years. According to the diary of Rev. Frederick A. O'Meara, in January 1845 the natives cut and squared the timbers for a church, and were assisted by the government workmen in raising the porch and steeple. In the fall of 1846, O'Meara travelled to England to raise funds to finish the church. His mission was successful and the church was completed late in 1848. In 1862, when the government discontinued most of its financial support, the native residents began moving north to Sheguiandah. In 1867 plans were made to relocate the church to Sheguiandah. This was a period of fiscal cutbacks, however, and the massive project was never undertaken. The settlement soon came to life again, following the beginning of island land sales in 1866.

St Paul's features three beautiful stained-glass windows created by Christopher Wallis, a well-known London, Ontario, artist. St Paul's graveyard is a reminder of Manitowaning's history as a government establishment. Buried here are Dr S. Layton (1813–66), a native of Kinross, Scotland, who was the Indian Department's doctor in Manitowaning for 17 years from 1849 to 1866, and his daughter Sarah, who died in 1858 at the age of 11.

East of St Paul's is the Manitowaning lighthouse, near which visitors have a panoramic view of Manitowaning Bay and the Wikwemikong Peninsula. Directly across the bay are the small native settlements of Two O'Clock and Buzwah. In 1884 John Waddell of Kingston began the construction of a number of lighthouses in this part of Ontario, including two on Manitoulin, one here and another at Cape Robert. Waddell failed to complete his contracts and the construction was taken over by the federal Department of Marine and Fisheries. The square wooden tower 11.5 metre (38 feet) high was put into operation in 1885. Benjamin Jones was the first keeper of the light, at an annual salary of $150.

For many years the tradition of an annual presentation of gifts to the natives was maintained at Manitowaning. This annual government-sponsored distribution to natives who had been war allies began after the War of 1812. Originally held at Drummond Island, then at Penetanguishene, the presentation moved to Manitowaning in 1836. The popular event was attended by 2,000 people in 1845 at a ceremony witnessed by

St Paul's Church is the oldest Anglican parish church in Northern Ontario.

artist Paul Kane. The tradition was officially discontinued by the government in 1855, but its spirit continued. On New Year's Day 1864 the Rev. Jabez Waters Sims, then resident Anglican clergyman, was visited by the local and Wikwemikong natives, to whom he gave gifts of provisions on behalf of himself and the government representative. As late as January 1880, the local paper recorded that 'the natives from Wikwemikong arrived as usual yesterday to receive presents from the merchants.'

Head west on Wellington Street out of town and turn right onto Highway 6. The first road on the left leads to Sucker Lake First Nation (Reserve No. 25). By 1868 most Manitowaning native residents had moved north to Sheguiandah. For those who wished to remain, this reserve containing 275 ha (680 acres) of good-quality land was created. The band's peak population of forty to fifty people had decreased to about a dozen by the turn of the century, after some of its Catholic members moved to Wikwemikong. Near Sucker Lake is the homestead of J.-B. Assiginack, for whom the township is named.

About 3 km (2 miles) north of Manitowaning the Bidwell Road leads to the tour featured in the 'Manitou Lake' chapter.

Continue north on Highway 6 for a wonderful view of Manitowaning Bay. The rolling farmland features large barns raised on island stone foundations, snake fences, and shingled farm buildings. Some of the island's first industries were saw and shingle mills. Manitoulin cedar shingles had an excellent reputation for durability. The cedar's slow growth produced a denser and therefore longer-lasting product than the quick-growing trees found on Canada's west coast.

About 8 km (5 miles) north of Manitowaning is the High Falls picnic area. The waterfall is created by the Francis Brook, which flows out of Turtle Lake 4 km (2.4 miles) to the northwest and over a limestone gorge into Manitowaning Bay. The falls were originally known as Five Mile Point Falls. Typical of the island's waterfalls, the stream flows over a limestone cap and drops sharply over a series of shale and limestone beds.

As you continue north through this farming belt note the flat fields littered with rocks and stumps, reminders of the pioneer challenge of land clearing. The rock piles scattered through the

High Falls

fields were hand-picked or 'plugged' by entire families attempting to clear their fields for crops.

This is Sheguiandah Township, established in 1864. It is the only island township to be given a native place name. Sheguiandah has several meanings, including 'home of the stork,' 'home of the Seguin,' and 'bay of grey slate.' According to Rev. J. Edward O'Flaherty, SJ, a specialist in native languages, one of the first two translations is the most likely. It is said that a native named the Stork and a Frenchman named Seguin lived here and provided shelter for travellers. 'Stork' in the Odawa language is 'shage,' and 'home of' is 'endah.'

On the west side is the Manitoulin East Municipal Airport, which opened in 1988. It is one of two Manitoulin airports. At the tip of this northerly stretch of highway is one of Ontario's most spectacular viewpoints – Ten Mile Point Lookout, with its breathtaking view of a thousand square miles of North Channel islands. Below the promontory, created by a bend in the Niagara Escarpment, lie the bays and islands of the North Channel set against a background of the white quartzite La Cloche Mountains on the distant North Shore. There is a small park, a picnic ground, and an art and craft shop with unique Manitoulin souvenirs such as the M'Chigeeng Native Creations' hand-made moccasins. The site also has historical significance. A plaque commemorates the 1648–50 Jesuit mission of Father Joseph Poncet to the resident Algonquian-speaking natives. Poncet was the first European resident of 'Ile-de-Ste-Marie' or 'Ekaentoton.' Although the actual location of the mission has not been confirmed, this is the most likely site. Wikwemikong and Manitowaning also lay claim to the distinction. The next permanent island residents settled almost two centuries later, around 1833 at Wikwemikong.

Cyclists are coming up on one of the island's larger hills. The Ten Mile Point hill heading south on Highway 6 is 1620 m (5500 feet) long with a 5 per cent grade.

At Ten Mile Point visitors can see a typical 'cement house,' now a rare form of house construction. The island is believed to have the country's largest concentration of intact cement homes. Across the highway from the point is the large square-planned Halcrow house. The James Halcrow family settled in a log

Ten Mile Point

house here in 1876. In May 1878 James purchased this 123-acre lot from the Indian Department at fifty cents per acre, for a total price of $61.50. James (1837–1906) emigrated to Canada from the Shetland Islands, Scotland, in 1868. He was joined several years later by his wife, Theresa Helen Hale Nicholson, and their three children. This now-abandoned home was built by James's descendants. For more information about cement house construction you may wish to consult consult chapter 5 on Manitoulin architecture.

John Meyers, his wife, Elizabeth Ponting, and their six children settled at Ten Mile Point in 1878. They arrived from Norfolk County, Ontario, followed shortly after by the four Trimmer brothers (George, Joseph, Thomas, and William) and Ambrose Abbott, his wife, Elizabeth Trimmer, and their family from York County, all of whom settled nearby.

Leaving Ten Mile Point drive due west for about 4 km (2.4 miles) to Sheguiandah First Nation (Reserve No. 24). The water on the right is Sheguiandah Bay, and the three sharp points of

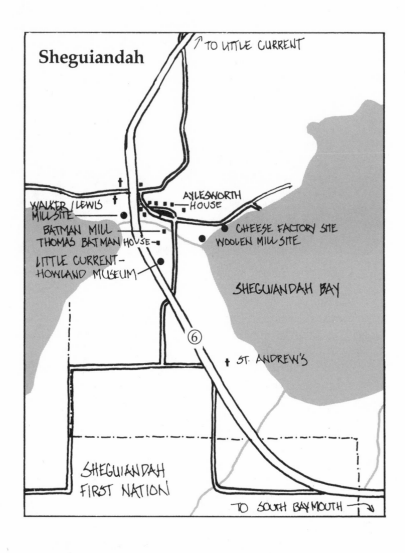

land projecting into the bay are named for three Anglican missionaries who worked with the natives in the earliest years of settlement. The southernmost, Sims Point, is named for Rev. Jabez Waters Sims (1831–69), known as Mkade-cunesse or 'Little Blackcoat.' He was missionary to the natives and settlers from 1864 until his death by drowning in 1869. He is buried across the road from the reserve, above the point. O'Meara Point, on the north side of the bay, is named for Rev. Frederick A. O'Meara. He was stationed at Manitowaning but was also active here from 1841 to 1859. O'Meara was called Tatebawad or 'He Who Walks on Water.' The northernmost tip of the bay is marked by Frost Point, named for Rev. Canon Frederick Frost, whose territory from 1877 to 1893 included Manitoulin and the North Shore.

Sheguiandah First Nation (Reserve No. 24) was formally established around 1866 when the native residents elected to remain after the 1862 treaty. With just over 2,023 ha (5,000 acres) it is the second largest island reserve, although only about one-third of the land is actually cultivable. Sheguiandah is currently undergoing a cultural rebirth. In 1990 the band held their first traditional powwow. The powwow is held in a picturesque location, nestled among trees on the shores of the bay next to the century-old church, and is well worth attending.

In 1864 Chief Edahwe Kezis lived here with ten families totalling forty-six people. Chief Kezis was born around 1813 in Upper Canada and lived here with his wife until his death in 1880. In 1867 he was joined by Chief Mizhequongi and his band from Manitowaning, bringing the total number of families to about twenty-nine. Chief Mizhequongi was born around 1806 in Upper Canada, and lived here with his wife, his son Albert, and family.

On the edge of the reserve on the east side of the highway is St Andrew's Anglican Church. The first church here was built in 1867 by the natives under the direction of the missionary Jabez Waters Sims. It was a log church and school building with a tinned tower surmounted by a cross. It remained unfinished for several years through lack of funds, though services and classes were conducted, with the carpenter's bench serving as both pulpit and desk. The log building was considered temporary and plans were made to relocate Manitowaning's St Paul's building here. St Paul's had been built 20 years earlier and some felt the building should follow its congregation to Sheguiandah. Funds were unavailable for the relocation project and the temporary log structure remained in service for about 20 years.

The present church, a picturesque white wood-frame building set in a clearing, was built in 1886. This church is unique as it was built entirely by the native community under the direction of missionary Frederick Frost. In 1998 Clara Waindubence initiated the process of turning the historic church building into a religious and cultural museum. The unique, unadorned interior features two sculptures by Simon Esquimaux. Its wood stove is a relic of the original 1867 church; it was transported to the island in the 1860s by Sims for his congregation.

St Andrew's Church has served the native community since 1886.

Sheguiandah in 1865 was in the process of transition, the natives torn between maintaining the traditional lifestyle and adopting the drastically different habits, homes, and livelihoods of European culture. While Sheguiandah was a permanent camp, the natives still made seasonal migrations to sugar camps and fishing and hunting grounds. At the same time they were forced to adopt log houses, a new religion, and agriculture. In May 1865 Sheguiandah's incumbent missionary, Sims, was witness to this difficult period when Margaret Mizhequongi, the daughter of Manitowaning's chief, died and was buried. When Sims arrived he found the grave of this very devout Anglican woman prepared in a traditional manner, with an axe, paddle, pipe, tobacco, corn, and bread (which Mrs Sims had sent) hung over the grave on a stick, along with painted flags and a staff. A nearby grave, of the son of Sheguiandah chief Edahwe Kezis, possessed a traditional wigwamace, a split-cedar board house over the grave surrounded by a cedar picket fence. The wigwamace also contained an axe, paddle, two small sleighs, two boats, a pipe, some tobacco, Indian corn, sugar cakes, and a small flag. The natives in attendance had blackened their faces with ash to ward off spirits. Discussion revealed that, while they had adopted the Anglican ways, they still maintained some of their deeply held traditional spiritual beliefs.

North of the reserve is the village of Sheguiandah. The Little Current–Howland museum has developed a walking tour from its grounds through town, if you don't mind a short hike. The museum contains many pioneer artefacts and is opened daily from mid-May to mid-September. A large museum building, barns, houses, granary, sugar shack, blacksmith shop, picnic ground, and washrooms are located in a pretty park setting. After visiting the museum, head into 'Sheg' for a quick tour.

Across the highway from Garrett's Motel near the museum is the Lewis Twin Peaks Trail. This 2-km trail near Bass Lake features quartzite rock, a marsh, an osprey viewing area, unusual plants like the hog peanut, found near the lake shore, moosewood or striped maple trees (named for their striped bark), and oak, ash, and ironwood trees. The trail is named for its two peaks overlooking Bass Lake and the North Channel, as well as for brothers David and Robert Lewis, who settled at Sheguiandah around 1866 and purchased this land in 1874. This is one of two trails opened in Howland Township in 1994, through the generosity of island residents. Please help preserve Manitoulin by staying on the paths and picking up litter.

Near Sheguiandah village is the site of an ancient quartz quarry and workshop site, one of the oldest discovered in North America. In the 1950s it was examined by Thomas Lee of the National Museum of Canada. His team found projectile points in the upper layer of soil, implements in a layer of glacial till, and stone implements beneath the till possibly 75,000 to 125,000 years old. He and several colleagues agreed humans had lived in the area during or before the last glaciation 30,000 years ago. These dates are still argued in archaeological circles. In 1992 Dr Peter Stork of the Royal Ontario Museum dated the quarry's occupation at between 10,000 BC and 7500 BC, or the first period after the glacial ice retreated. The 86-acre site is a protected private area but many archaeological objects can be seen at the Centennial Museum of Sheguiandah.

The village of Sheguiandah was settled following the 1862 treaty because of its potential for water power. The stream which runs from Bass Lake to the bay was powering three mills by 1902, a grist mill, a saw and shingle mill, and a woollen mill. The first mill, a water-driven grist mill, was built in 1871 by Joseph Walker, the founder of Walkerton, Ontario. Walker, who was born in Tyrone, Ireland, around 1807, emigrated with his parents to Canada in 1827. He was apparently unsuccessful in his business ventures, and to better his fortunes he moved to Manitoulin late in life. The mill was purchased by David Lewis and remained in his son James's family until 1958, when it was removed for highway improvements. It was situated on the northwest corner of the intersection of Highway 6 and the river.

The second mill was located on the site of the present-day Batman's mill replica. William H. Becks built a saw and shingle mill here in 1879. In the fall of 1879 it was purchased by David Lewis's brother Robert, and in 1889 it was sold to Thomas James Batman (1851–1941), who operated it until around 1940. The site features a scaled-down replica of the mill and its water flume, a flat rock riverbed, and a small dam. Upstream from the mill a wooden footbridge leads to Batman's former home. Batman was born in Liverpool, England, and settled on Manitoulin in 1877. Like many island bachelors, he married a woman who came to Manitoulin to teach, in this case Evangeline Agnew from the Bidwell School.

The third mill was located on the north side of the river's mouth. A woollen mill was opened in 1902 by Ezra Hallman and operated by Harry Weber. Its establishment was made possible by a $500 municipal bonus granted by Howland Township. It ran until the early 1920s. On the bay, just north of the woollen mill, was a cheese factory built by Adam Trotter in the 1890s and operated by Charles Aylesworth (1851–1931), who was said to be the best cheese-maker in Ontario. North of the cheese factory was a fishing station operated by John Hastie, as well as a government dock, a wharf, and a lighthouse. The post

Batman's sawmill replica

office was established here in 1874 and operated by David Lewis. In 1879 the settlement's first hotel was built by Thomas English. By 1882 Sheguiandah boasted a store, blacksmith shop, new school, and brickyard. Two years later it became the first island village to have a brass band. Sheguiandah was a bustling community 90 years ago.

Across Mill Street from the footbridge are John Hastie's home, which was built around 1900, his wife's millinery shop, and on the corner, an earlier Hastie residence and store. John Hastie came from Quebec to Little Current to work as a blacksmith, but became a fisherman in the 1890s with partners James Noble and Hector Roszel. Around 1896 he moved to Sheguiandah with his wife, Margaret Roszel, to establish his own fish station with Fred Foreshaw. He built a dock and net shed on the bay, as well as these buildings on Mill Street.

A walk through the village takes you past Charles Aylesworth's Robert Street residence, built around 1900. In the summer the hillside of this pretty home is covered in giant hollyhocks. If you drive down Mill and Dunlop streets, along the north shore of the bay, you will come to a small picnic area, boat launch, and government dock with a view of the bay's opposite shore.

On the west side of Highway 6 on the Green Bay Road are the village's churches. On the south side is the Sheguiandah United (formerly Methodist) Church, finished in 1894. This, the second church on the site, replaced a twenty-year-old church. In 1949 the Honora United Church building was moved here to become the church hall. On the north side is St Peter's Anglican Church, built in 1883. Visitors to Sheguiandah First Nation and the adjacent village are often curious about the number of churches, and in particular why there are two Anglican churches, both dating from the 1880s. The answer lies in the area's history. When the churches were built two large and distinct communities existed, both served by the same minister. St Peter's village church served the non-native residents, while St Andrew's services were conducted in the native language.

The Green Bay Road, a favourite shortcut, travels past century-old farms to Cup and Saucer Hill and West Bay. The island's second oil boom occurred at the Pike Lake and Green Bay settlements in 1886. Like the 1864 discoveries at Wikwemikong, Maple Point, Strawberry Island, West Bay, Mindemoya, and Howland, the exploration and excitement were short-lived. Oil interests were revived and extinguished periodically.

From the village, turn north onto Highway 6; on the northeast corner is a large painted cement house built early in this century. On the right is a silica quarry. A high grade of silica rock was extracted in the 1940s and 1950s from an outcropping of quartzite rock that emerged above the limestone. The silica was used for coating bathroom fixtures and making cooking utensils.

Two km north of the museum on the west side of Highway 6 is the Orr Mountain Hiking Trail. The Wayne Orr family trail is on land purchased by Arthur and Sara Orr in 1879. This trail is 3.5 km in length and takes about one and one-half hours to hike. Two lookout points provide great views of the silica quarry, Sheguiandah Bay, Strawberry Channel, and the North Shore. Be sure to note the varied vegetation, including many hawberry or hawthorn bushes (distinguished by their berries and very long thorns) near the eastern lookout. Wild raspberry and strawberry plants can be found near the hardwood forest. Trilliums, lady-slippers, and chicory are abundant. In the sky look for turkey vultures, broad-winged hawks, blue jays, and purple finches.

East of the highway on the right is the Sheguiandah United Church cemetery. The earliest stone belongs to John Atkinson, who died in 1886 aged 59. John had followed his brother Francis (1843–1927) to Manitoulin. Natives of Blackwatertown, Ireland, they homesteaded here in 1866. Francis married Eliza Jane Stringer, an Irish-born woman living in Orangeville, Ontario. It appears that Atkinson persuaded the entire Stringer family to settle on the island as well.

Continuing north you will have a beautiful view of Straw-berry Channel and Strawberry Island, also known as Appiss-abikokaning, or 'at the place where there is an abundance of violet-coloured stones.' This large island stretches almost from Sheguiandah to Little Current. A lighthouse was established in 1881 on the northern tip of the island after a large number of ships were wrecked in the vicinity. The first summer homes on Manitoulin were built on Strawberry in 1880. According to the local newspaper, J.H. Hawkes got a contract to erect 'rustic houses' there for two residents of Guelph, Ontario. Strawberry Island's cedar forests are a wintering ground for eastern Manitoulin's deer population.

The highway from Sheguiandah to Little Current was constructed in 1866–8. The original road meandered more than the present highway, avoiding rock cuts and the highest hills where possible. The hill opposite Strawberry Island is Burnett Hill, named for James Burnett who settled here in 1866. For a pretty side trip, turn left on the Green Bush Road, and then take the first right to McLean's Mountain lookout, which is just southwest of Little Current. The route crosses a plateau of grazing land, and both the beginning and end of this detour feature dramatic coastal views. Nearby Strawberry Channel Viewpoint is a great spot to pause and enjoy the scenery of Strawberry Island, Ten Mile Point, and the Wikwemikong Peninsula. This quiet spot was donated in memory of Bob Brailey by his family.

Continue north on Highway 6 past White's Point on the east, named for George White, who with his wife, Maribah Sickles, and their son Darius, from Uxbridge, Ontario, purchased this land in 1868. This is now a small community of summer and permanent residents.

A typical settler's residence could, at best, be described as a shanty. We often picture quaint pioneer cabins as comparable to the cottage-country versions created today. In fact, the cabins provided minimal shelter. Rev. Jabez Sims recorded that his own residence often 'filled with drifting snow several times' in a day, and that he would waken 'to find everything including the bread frozen solid.'

In November 1864 Sims, with John Burkitt, the Little Current schoolmaster, Donald McDonald, a politician who was touring the island, and Willie Abbotossway, guide and interpreter, visited Henry Charles Fraser, one of Howland Township's early non-native pioneers. He had homesteaded in 1864 about 5 km (3 miles) southwest of Little Current. Sims gave the following account of Fraser's early homestead:

November 7th 1864 – The Honourable D. McDonald, being
wind-bound, started out with me and Mr. Burkitt to visit the new

settler Mr. Fraser and an Indian, Ishkemah, about 3 miles from the
Little Current back in the woods. We passed through some stony
land for about a mile back when we came to some good land. We
observed that the fire had done much damage: no animals to be
seen either rabbits or partridges. We called at Ishkemah's – but
found that he had gone out hunting. I found his wife and 6 children at home. George's little boy Willie [Abbotossway] interpreted for me – I promised to call on returning. We travelled
through the Indian gardens which we found had been seriously
damaged by the late fires, and at length came upon Fraser's
shanty. A small building about 6 feet square with a clay floor. He
was engaged in stopping up the crevices between the logs with
clay. The little log cabin is covered with a trough roof. [A trough or
scoop roof is built of logs split in half lengthwise and hollowed
out like a trough. A row of troughs is laid hollow side up, then a
second layer is laid on top hollow side down.] He is all alone
here – he is therefore his own cook, baker, washerwoman and
everything else. He has but one companion, a faithful dog. He told
us that he was much pleased with the land, and that he expected
his relations up in the Spring. He has taken up 200 acres of excellent land; the land here is of the very best description sandy loam
and clay bottom the very best for farming purposes. We were very
good naturedly invited to partake of a dinner of boiled fish and
potatoes which being hungry we gladly accepted. But how were
we all to be disposed of in an apartment not more than 6 feet
square, and without the encumbrances of chairs or table? Two
boxes and a bench were brought into requisition. A piece of split
basswood fastened to the side of the shanty by 2 pegs served for a
table and we then sat down to our dinner. I was honoured with
the best knife in the establishment. Mr McD used his pocket knife
and Mr B was furnished with an old disk knife. We were supplied
with wooden forks (sticks after the Chinese fashion). However we
ate a hearty meal, washing down our fish and potatoes with a
pannikin of tea each. Our host was evidently pleased with our
visit. After dinner I made a few remarks – exhorting him not to
forget the one thing needful. He tells me he has a New Testament –
I promised to give him a Bible when I come again. He has a rifle, a
shotgun, a pistol and a bowie knife – so that he is well armed
against enemies either human or otherwise. He accompanied us

through his land (i.e. his in prospect for it is not yet in the market) and he certainly has made an excellent selection. Here is as good land as any I have seen in Canada, good deep soil and fine hardwood timber. There is room here for a very good settlement. We went to the top of the ridge, a little to the south (say 1/2 mile) of Fraser's shanty, where we had a beautiful prospect – we could see across the Island, the Current and the La Cloche Mountains. On returning we came to a beautiful waterfall of about 20 feet over which the swamp on the top of the ridge empties itself into a perennial stream which empties itself into the Lake – but owing to the excessive drought this summer it is now dried up. We now bade farewell to our friend who is now left alone in the woods and started for the Little Current: on our way we called at Ishkemah's but found that he had not returned. I read a Psalm, offered prayer and we then returned to the Current, highly pleased with our days excursion.

ELEVEN

Mindemoya Lake
(Tour 4)

The central shortcut from the village
of West Bay (M'Chigeeng) through
Mindemoya to the island's most beautiful
beach at Providence Bay

This scenic route connects the northern and southern tours
mid-way, and is ideal for those who have limited time to tour.
From either Little Current or South Baymouth visitors may follow a shortened circle tour which includes the eastern bays; the
north coast as far as West Bay or M'Chigeeng, a native cultural
centre; Mindemoya, the centre of the island; Providence Bay
and its beach; then back to South Baymouth or Little Current
(160 km or 96 miles). The central shortcut from West Bay to
Providence Bay is only 26 km (15.5 miles), although you may
wish to spend more time experiencing the cultural and sports
activities. If weather permits, allow some time to lounge on
Providence Bay's beautiful sand beach, where it is still not
uncommon to find yourself the sole sun-worshipper.

Begin at the junction of Highways 540 and 551, and follow
Highway 551 south from the native village of West Bay or
M'Chigeeng past Mindemoya Lake. Beside the lake is a small
shoreside picnic area. Mindemoya Lake is the island's third
largest lake (Manitou and Kagawong are larger), about 12 km
(7 miles) long and 7 km (4 miles) wide. Nearly 30.5 metres
(100 feet) higher than Lake Huron, it is located near the geographic centre of the island. The name Mindemoya (Mndimooy-
enh) refers to the island located directly west of the picnic area,

WEST BAY

BOWSER'S CORNER

540

KAGAWONG
LAKE

WEST BAY

WEST BAY
FIRST NATION

HIKING
TRAIL

MINDEMOYA

HIKING TRAIL

CAVE •

MINDEMOYA OR TREASURE
ISLAND

LAKE

551

MINDEMOYA

542

DRYDEN'S CORNER

MEMORIAL

C A R N A R V O N

MINDEMOYA R.

PROVIDENCE
BAY

LAKE HURON
Mindemoya Lake

Mindemoya Island

which resembles an old woman on her hands and knees. Several native legends explain the presence of this old woman. Kitche Manitou (the Great Spirit), creator of the universe, sent Nanabush, the son of a human mother and spirit father, to teach the Anishnaabeg. Nanabush, who was raised by his grandmother, possessed supernatural powers, including the power of transformation. Nanabush was running from the south, according to one legend, with his grandmother over his shoulder. She was heavy, but he got this far when he stumbled and lost his balance. His grandmother flew through the air, landing on her hands and knees in the middle of the lake, where she remains. He continued on his journey, stopping at Cup and Saucer Hill to rub the magic alder bushes against his cuts and bruises. The alders turned red from his blood, and remain red to this day.

Another version of the story tells how the wife of Nanabush ran away from him, travelling up the Bruce Peninsula onto Manitoulin, where she settled on an island in Mindemoya Lake.

Nanabush searched the North Shore and Manitoulin for her, leaving a trail of excellent hunting grounds wherever he passed. When he arrived at West Bay (M'Chigeeng) he sat down on the stone cliff forming Cup and Saucer Hill. He looked west and saw his wife on the island in Mindemoya Lake. In anger he said, 'You can stay there!' And she did.

In 1883 the island was purchased for $60.00 by the McPherson family of Toronto. In 1928 the McPhersons sold the island to Joe and Jean Hodgson, who operated the renowned 'Treasure Island' tourist camp for many years. Jean (1903–94) wrote a fascinating history of their lives on this isolated island.

Enjoy the view of the island, and the lake, from any of several viewpoints. There is a particularly beautiful vista at sunset. This is the first of three picnic areas on the lake in the Mindemoya vicinity. Across the highway, Love's Cedar Cove Farm has stood for over a century.

This is Carnarvon Township, which was organized in 1879 with pioneers Francis (Frank) Wagg as reeve and his brother Colman as clerk. Carnarvon was named for Henry Howard Molyneux Herbert (1831–90), the fourth earl of Carnarvon. Carnarvon, Sandfield, and Campbell Townships formed the Township of Central Manitoulin in 1998. You may take the Ketchankookem Trail to the Carnarvon Municipal park and the Brookwood Brae golf course.

Drive to the centre of town to the intersection of Highways 551 and 542 to park. Mindemoya is called the hub of the island. It currently has a population of about five hundred. Mindemoya's success can be attributed to its central location and the good soils of the area. The community has many services, including a grocery store, restaurants, a hardware store, a bank, and several gift shops. Mindemoya celebrates an annual homecoming weekend on the Canada Day holiday. The Central Manitoulin Lions Club Fiddler's Jamboree is held annually, with fiddlers from across Ontario competing. There is fishing for the lake's pickerel and whitefish, as well as bass, northern pike, and perch.

Settlers began arriving in the Mindemoya area in 1875. The hamlet's future was secured in October 1879 when John Morrison established a general store and Alexander Howell opened a grist, saw, and shingle mill 5 km (3 miles) to the southwest. John Morrison settled here at the age of 24, accompanied by his wife, Ida. The following spring, Kinnear and Jones set up a black-smith and wagon-making shop opposite Morrison's store.

That same spring stonemason and farmer Francis Wagg (1845–1927) became the first postmaster. Francis arrived around 1877 from Goodwood, Ontario, where his father Tom Wagg had settled in 1836 from Norfolk, England. Francis and his wife, Elizabeth Cooke, raised nine children in Mindemoya. By December 1880 the hamlet was dubbed 'Morrisonia' by the local paper. In 1884–5 the *Ontario Gazetteer and Business Directory* counted a population of thirty, with two churches (Presbyterian and Methodist), a school, and N. Elliott's sawmill.

On Highway 551 at Hare's Creek, the Central Manitoulin Historical Society has set up Pioneer Park, featuring a log cabin museum and covered bridge.

Mindemoya is the home and birthplace of Manitoulin's dairy industry, founded by A.J. Wagg (1875–1960), the son of Francis and Elizabeth Wagg. It was operated by his family until 1981, when the business was purchased by Farquhar's Dairy. The Wagg family had been known in the Goodwood vicinity for their progressive farms, credited to their English farming background. The Farquhars were also island pioneers. Settling near Kagawong in 1877 were William Sr, who had been born in Wick, Scotland, in 1845, his Irish wife, Jane Nixon, and their ten children. The stone dairy building located at the intersection of Highways 551 and 542 downtown was built around 1902 and rebuilt in 1931 following a fire. Kitty-corner from the dairy building, the corner grocery was built in 1899 for W.J. McKenzie, who sold out to Frank Wagg the following year.

East of the dairy are the municipal building, United Church, Waggs Woods, and the Jack Seabrook farm museum. The municipal complex building was built as a school in 1921, from local limestone. Waggs Woods, south of the municipal building, is a 49-acre site on the farm of pioneer Francis Wagg and his son A.J. Wagg. The forest is home to basswood, maple, birch, and ash, as well as countless wild flowers and fern. A highlight is the rare moon seed vine. The United Church was built in 1918.

Jack Seabrook's Agricultural Museum is located on Highway

The Anglican Church of Saint Francis of Assisi

542 east of the dairy corner. It contains Northern Ontario's largest private collection of pre-war farm machinery. The museum is open from the end of May through Thanksgiving.

Two blocks west of the dairy corner is the Anglican Church of Saint Francis of Assisi. Its most striking feature is its stone 'Norman'-styled entrance tower. The church opened on 25 July 1935, following two years of community labour inspired by the town's first resident clergyman, Rev. Richard Martin Taylor. Before this time the community hall had been used for services. The Toronto architectural firm of Molesworth, West, and Secord designed the building. The church is constructed entirely of island materials, including the heavy oak and maple beams, limestone, and lime from local kilns. All the window sashes, frames, doors, and even the stairs, pulpit, and furnishings were hand-made by members of the congregation. An informative brochure, available for a small donation, describes in detail the church as well as the historical treasures it contains. These include priceless sixteenth-century silk curtains embroidered with gold threads, owned by Queen Elizabeth I. The curtains originally hung beside the altar in the Kensington Palace Royal Chapel. Candlesticks from King Charles I of England (1625–49) rest on the credence table, and a twelfth-century sculpture of an angel from the Palace of Westminster stands above the altar. The church treasures were obtained through the fundraising efforts of English-born Rev. Richard Martin Taylor, who formed the Society of Friends of St Francis. The society contacted former parishioners, as well as patrons throughout Canada and Britain. Some of the benefactors included the Hon. G. Howard Ferguson, high commissioner of Canada; Prime Minister R.B. Bennett; and Rev. Canon H.J. Cody, president of the University of Toronto. The church also boasts several beautiful stained-glass windows created by the Toronto studio of McCausland.

Highway 542/551 heading west passes Mindemoya's former medical centre: the large brick building on the right, which now contains offices, was the island's first hospital. In 1920 Dr Robert Davis built it as a private hospital. Davis had been operating a small clinic in the farmhouse to the west since 1910. When Dr Davis retired from Manitoulin for health reasons in 1934, the community petitioned the Red Cross to take over his hospital. Funds were raised to purchase the hospital from Dr Davis, and it was operated by the Red Cross until 1980. In 1970 a new building, located at the north end of town, was constructed. Ten years later the Mindemoya Red Cross Hospital and Little Current's Manitoulin Health Centre were amalgamated.

Davis's former farmhouse and clinic buildings now house Hope Farm, established in 1979 as a residence and workplace for the mentally handicapped. The buildings were renovated to accommodate eight permanent residents and up to eighteen day workers. Many products are for sale, including wooden lawn furniture.

On the right is Mindemoya Lake. The township's first mill was established in this area, known as Hopetown, in 1879. In October 1879 the Carnarvon Township council granted a bonus of $1,000 to Alexander Howell of Manitowaning to aid in the construction of a grist, saw, and shingle mill on Colman Wagg's property on Lake Mindemoya. In January 1880 Howell opened

The Monument Corner war memorial was dedicated in 1921.

his saw and shingle mill, followed in June by a grist mill, both the products of the township's deal. Howell, who had been born in Ontario about 1838, settled here with his wife, Alice, and their seven children.When the mill burned down in December 1883 the community mourned the loss of the mill as well as the township's $1,000 investment.

Just west of the lake is Monument Corner, also known as the Four Corners or Alexander's Corner. In 1921 a statue of a soldier was placed here in honour of the local men who fought and died in the First World War. The statue was originally located in the middle of the intersection, but it was damaged by a motorist and the remains of the memorial were relocated to the present site on the southwest corner around 1960. A neighbour, George White, donated the site, and a spire replaced the damaged marble soldier. The current monument and park are the result of several years of island-wide fundraising in the 1990s. In June 1994 the site was rededicated as the Manitoulin District Cenotaph to honour the 130 men who gave their lives in the two world wars, the Korean War, and the Vietnam War. Monument Corner is the site of the original island-wide Decoration Day celebration. Beginning in the 1920s, according to First World War veteran Bill Sims, 'on Decoration Day we (veterans and citizens alike) would go all the way around the island, starting at Wikwemikong and ending at Spring Bay where we held a combined service.' A number of former soldiers formed the Great War Veterans Association in April 1917. By 1919 it was the largest such group in the country; the Little Current WVA received its charter on 12 May 1919. This group and other similar organizations came together and formed the Canadian Legion of the British Empire Service League in 1926, which was renamed the Royal Canadian Legion in 1960.

At Monument Corner you may take a short detour north to the Mindemoya Lake Cave located at the Rock Garden Terrace Resort. About 3 km (2 miles) north of Monument Corner is the former community of Old Spring Bay. Today this is a small summer community, but in 1880, during the settlement boom, thirty-five families lived in the immediate vicinity. In 1897, twenty years after homesteading here, Benjamin Back was named the first postmaster of Spring Bay, or Cavemount, as the

Mindemoya Lake Cave

community was temporarily called. Continue past Old Spring Bay along Mindemoya Lake to the limestone cave.

In the mid-1950s Frank A. Myers studied and wrote about the history of this cave. On 21 September 1888 three Mennonite preachers, Daniel Hagey of Waterloo, William Schroeder, founder of the Spring Bay Mennonite Church, and John Evans of Manitoulin, were fishing without success and decided to shoot ducks instead. They discovered the cave while looking for a fallen duck. The floor was littered with about fifteen skeletons, presumed to be Huron natives who were slaughtered by the Iroquois during their raids in the mid-1600s. The skeletons were sent to the old University of Toronto museum, but were subsequently destroyed by fire. The cave is located 5 metres (15 feet) below the top of the bluff, and 17 metres (50 feet) above water. It ranges from 4.5 to 3 metres (15 to 9 feet) in height and is about 23 metres (75 feet) deep, with several bends and passages. The limestone cave was formed by water erosion after the last glaciers receded, about 10,000 years ago.

In 1989 London *Free Press* travel writer David Scott declared the Rock Garden Terrace Resort one of the five best lodgings in Ontario, partly for its scenic location and fabulous view from the limestone cliff overlooking Mindemoya Lake. Owner Oswald Argmann is justifiably proud of his achievement, as well as the restoration of the cave. For a small admission charge visitors can explore the cave.

About 1 km north of the cave is the Carnarvon–Billings Line hiking trail. The entrance is on the west side of the road and is marked by a sign. There is limited parking on the road's shoulder. The 2.5 km (1.5 mile) trail heads due west along the township line, following old logging roads. It rises through hardwood forest to the island's flat dolomite rock, which is scattered with typical second-growth forest. The main trail ends at the power line. It is considered to be an easy, dry trail.

Return south to Highway 551, turning west at Monument Corner. Drive 2 km (a little over 1 mile) and then turn south to Providence Bay, which is described in the Southern Route chapter.

TWELVE

Around Manitou Lake
(Tour 5)

This tour through picturesque farm communities circles Manitoulin's largest lake. It provides many glimpses of and opportunities to visit the lake. It takes half a day to drive this route equipped with a picnic lunch; otherwise allow a little extra time for a meal in Manitowaning, Sandfield, or Mindemoya. Manitou Lake is a good spot to catch smallmouth bass, yellow perch, and lake trout.

This tour begins in Manitowaning, although it is possible to start at Sheguiandah, West Bay, Mindemoya, or South Baymouth. From Manitowaning head north on Highway 6 for 3.5 km (2 miles), then turn left towards Bidwell and Green Bay at the signs 'Bidwell Road' and 'to Highway 540.'

Within 1 km the road begins to wind northwest. Follow the paved surface and watch for the numerous abrupt turns. The side road to Holiday Haven resort leads to the former lakeshore community of Vanzant's Landing, also known as Budge's Settlement. John Budge, a Scottish boat builder, his wife, Elizabeth, and family, and Henry Vanzant, an American-born farmer, and his family settled here in 1871 and 1874 respectively. John Budge supported his family for a few years by working in the timber mills at Michael's Bay on the south shore, then later returned to his boat-building trade. Vanzant's Landing was a primary stop

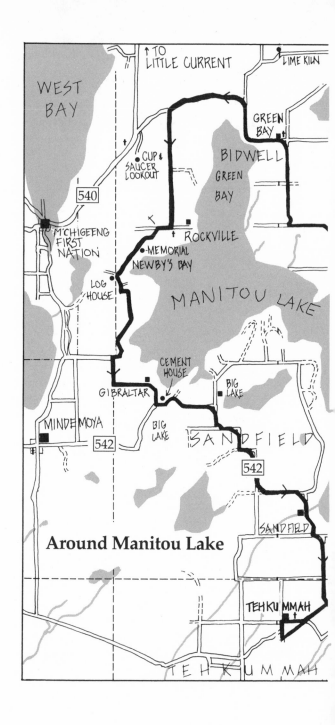

Around Manitou Lake

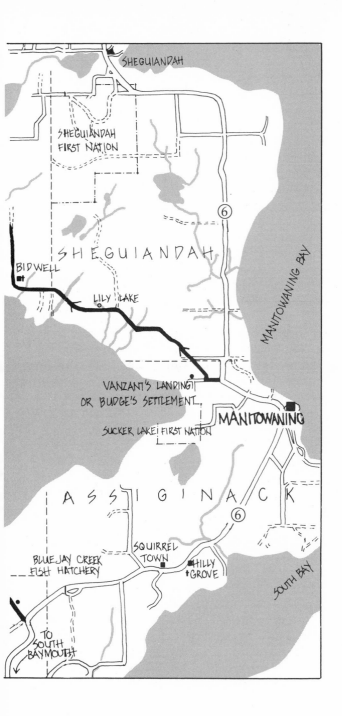

on the Lake Manitou ferry routes. By the late 1880s, ferries such as Robert Stapleton's *Della S.* were carrying settlers and supplies to shops at Lehman's Landing, Sprys, Bassingthwaightes, Birch Point, Paul's Point, McDonald's Mills, and Plant's Bay. Around 1888 Robert Stapleton built a sawmill, which was later replaced by a mill belonging to the Stoddard, Maitland, and Rixon Company of Owen Sound, Ontario. The settlement's cement-block school is located on the north side of the road. Past the school, the road leaves Assiginack Township and enters Sheguiandah Township. Sheguiandah has several translations, the most plausible of which are 'home of the stork' and 'home of the Seguin,' named either for a native or a Frenchman.

One hundred and fifty years ago Manitou Lake was the centre of the native transportation system. By the mid-1840s native settlements could be found in at least a dozen locations on the island's Lake Huron shores. All these settlements were connected by water routes and rough trails. At the centre of these routes was Manitou Lake, over which everyone travelled when moving from points east to coastal camps north and west. The island's first European settlers also made use of these efficient routes, often counting a crude boat among their most prized possessions. The lake, like Manitoulin itself, is named for the Kitche Manitou, or Great Spirit.

The area southeast of Manitou Lake was settled from 1866 to 1876, shortly after the eastern portion of Manitoulin. From Manitowaning along Manitou Lake's northeastern shore to Green Bay you are travelling on one of the island's first roads. The section from Manitowaning to the lake was known as the Lake Manitou portage road. By 1881 this 6 km (3.5 mile) trail was passable, but considered incomplete. The next 10 km (6 miles) of the lake section which you follow to Green Bay, known as the Lake Manitou Road, was constructed in 1880 and within a few years was a heavily travelled route to the west and north.

Many cedar-rail snake fences are found along this route. A tiny private cemetery is located on the left. An old shingled farmhouse and its log barn stand on the right. Like most pioneers, the island settlers constructed their homes and outbuildings of readily available, inexpensive materials – logs first, followed by lumber and shingles.

Just ahead, the big red Moggy family barn on the left and large cement farmhouse on the right mark the Lily Lake settlement. The post office opened here in 1880. Leaving this hamlet you pass the lake for which the community was named.

The road now heads northwest, following the shore of Manitou Lake, which is hidden behind the stoney bushland on the left. Hidden Springs Farm's tin-sided farm house was built in 1870 by George and Sadie (McArthur) Chatwell. Bidwell Township begins here, and after the sharp north turn is the hamlet of Bidwell.

Note here the white frame Bidwell United Church and the brick Bidwell School No. 4, which was built in 1913. The school is now a private residence, but is still surmounted by its bell. Charles Woodward, founder of western Canada's Woodward's retail chain, operated a small trading post here in 1875. After turning his initial investment of $500 into $2,000, he moved to the larger trading centre of Manitowaning to open a store. He remained on the island for twelve years, experiencing both boom and bust before heading west to found his empire. For more information on Woodward's career consult the Manitowaning section on the Eastern Bays tour.

About 2 km (1 mile) north of Bidwell the road jogs west again. One kilometre down the road stands another former church, constructed of red brick. The road runs through swampland, followed by rocky bushland, picturesque trees, and stones piled by pioneers. Imagine the work involved in picking up and carrying every single rock, a labour-intensive method of land clearing which involved all family members. The road turns west again for a short distance, past rail fences, more stone piles, and bush.

Although tourism had begun on the island by 1879, it did not really develop until around 1920 with the increased popularity of the automobile. The Manitou Lake area was second only to the island's shoreline in tourist appeal. The next 17 km (10 miles) lead to Rockville, circling Manitou Lake's largest bay, Green Bay. Turn west for a half-kilometre detour, towards Red Lodge, for views of the back of Cup and Saucer Hill, the island's highest point, and Green Bay.

Bidwell Township, which contains the northern portion of

Lake Manitou, was established in 1864 and is named for the Hon. Marshall Spring Bidwell, lawyer, politician, and Speaker of the House of Commons in the mid-1800s. In 1864 provincial land surveyor Joseph Hobson was less than impressed with Bidwell Township: 'I regret to say that I cannot speak very favourably of this township. By far the greater part of it consists of swamps, and poor, sandy and very rocky tracts of land, covered with a dense growth of timber principally evergreen. In many places it is broken by high and very steep hills and outcrops of rocks.' John Dunlop was the township's first settler. He arrived in 1866, homesteading at Pike Lake, near Sheguiandah, in the northeastern corner of the township. He was the sole landowner until June 1868, when he was joined by John Atkinson. Descendants of both pioneers still live on the island. A small oil boom occurred at Pike Lake in 1886. Wells were dug and stock sold, but the promised prosperity never came.

Drive north through more rolling bush, and watch for the sharp left turn to enter the community of Green Bay. The road straight through leads to Sheguiandah via Pike Lake. At the turn the community centre, a former one-room school, is on the right. Thomas J. Batman won the contract to build School Section No. 5 school in 1881. By August 1882, thirty students were being taught by Lindsay Ferguson. On your right was the Ferguson homestead. Lindsay Ferguson (1856–1914) and his wife, Sarah Ann Stringer (1861–1941), both settled on Manitoulin around 1870 with their respective families, married, and raised their children. In 1882 Sarah was the fortunate heir to a feather bed and $200, left to her by her mother, Elizabeth Stringer. More than a century later we may smile at the bed bequest, but this would have been a valuable asset and a creature comfort where few could be found. Elizabeth left a total of $600 in assets to be divided among her six children. Sarah, as the youngest and only unmarried child, received the largest amount of cash and one of the two beds, presumably as her future dowry. Elizabeth had previously bestowed sums of money or generous gifts upon her other children when they homesteaded or married. Her second son, James, received a team of horses when he homesteaded on the island.

The Green Bay post office opened in 1878 under the name of

Skippen's Settlement. The white-sided Green Bay United Church, which opened in 1892, was described by its first missionary as 'neat and commodious.' It was built for $700 and opened debt-free, a coveted status in pioneer communities. One year later the church was painted, and two years later a shed to shelter the horses was built and an organ was purchased. It was built by pioneer fundraising efforts, including tea meetings and neighbourly donations of materials and labour. In the adjacent cemetery are the graves of pioneers like the Skippen and Ferguson families. John Ferguson (1822–1920), born in New Brunswick of Irish stock, his wife, Mary Jane, and their four children, including Lindsay, whose home you just passed, settled here in 1870.

The Green Bay settlement has several cement houses in its vicinity, including two at the sharp right turn leaving Bidwell. Continue north 2 km (1 mile) from Green Bay to the first intersection, and turn sharply left. About half a kilometre north on this stretch is the site of the area's first church and cemetery, which was opened in 1882 by the Disciples of Christ and was later known as Skippen's Church. The Twin Cedars cemetery, marked today by a small wire fence, white gate, and Baptist Cemetery sign, contains the headstones of pioneers John Skippen (c 1815–90) and his wife, Elizabeth Ann. They moved here from Orangeville, Ontario, with their eight sons, daughter, and daughter-in-law in 1870. Straight ahead, the Skippen farm with its red-painted barn is visible. The farm has been in the Skippen family for more than a century.

To continue the Manitou Lake tour turn left. A short detour straight past the Skippen farm leads to a lime kiln and Sheguiandah by a picturesque route through rolling farmland. An original pioneer lime kiln is located 2 km (1 mile) north of the intersection, on private property. It is hidden by birch trees and some brush on a rise. Manitoulin is composed mainly of limestone rock, and lime (as calcium oxide) is an ingredient in cement. A number of local residents constructed lime kilns or firing ovens to extract lime from island rock. As early as 1879 kiln firings were announced in the local newspaper. A kiln firing was often a social event, with lunch, dancing, and music. The rocks were hauled to the kiln, which was essentially a large

A pioneer lime kiln

rock oven with mud-packed sides and a crude grate. The kiln was fired around the clock for about a week. Kilns varied in size from those producing about one hundred bushels to those producing four hundred bushels per firing. A bushel sold for about twenty-five cents. One very popular use of island lime was in the construction of cement houses, although the lime was also used extensively for fieldstone mortar and cement barn foundations. For more about barns and cement houses consult the architecture chapter of this book.

After turning left just before the Skippen farm, drive 3.5 km (2 miles) west, then turn south to Rockville. Watch for this turn, as it can easily be missed. If you wish to hike the island's highest peak, Cup and Saucer Hill, continue west for two more kilometres, rather than south to Rockville, and enjoy a panoramic two-hour hike on the Niagara Escarpment (fully described in the North Coast chapter).

Continuing south to Rockville the gravel road, lined with snake fences, travels through both bush and fields of Queen Anne's Lace and other wildflowers. The south road ends at the Memorial Hall, where you turn right and soon afterwards, left. The former Rockville Grace United Church, now the Memorial Hall, was built through community efforts. In 1920 Mrs Alfred (Lily) Spry, Wells Parkinson, and Alfred Newby formed a fund-raising committee which held concerts, socials, plays, and picnics. Nine years later construction began with largely donated labour and materials. The church was built by John McDermid of Providence Bay, assisted by Albert Sheppard Jr on land donated by Burn Spry. The project started Sheppard on a construction career. The first couple married here were Harvey Spry and Zella Newby (children of Burn Spry and Alfred Newby) on 10 September 1930. It was a union of the original fundraisers and landowners. Zella's family still lives on a nearby farm with their own family, whose industry and achievements continue to match those of their ancestors. The church closed in 1961, and was taken over by the community in 1963.

Rockville post office was established in 1900 with James Spry, a blacksmith, as postmaster. The second and final postmaster was his son Alfred Thomas Spry, who held the position from his father's death in 1921 until 1952. The Spry family, headed by James H. (1843–1921) and his wife, Sarah, were pioneers in the area. James, born in Ontario, and Sarah, born on Prince Edward Island, settled here around 1875 and raised nine children. Adam and Jane Demi and their three children, who later moved to the United States, were the first family to settle in the area. Other early settlers included Joshua and Mary Jane Parkinson, the Cannards, and Albert and Elisa Sheppard. Mrs Cannard used to pick cranberries in the deep bush behind Parkinson's, and was known for unwinding and winding a ball of yarn to find her way back through the bushes.

Heading west and south, away from Rockville and the lake, is another good view of Cup and Saucer Hill. If you pay close attention, about 2.5 km (1.5 miles) from Rockville you will see in the bush on the left side of the road a cobblestone memorial to

William McFall Martin (1913–31), a young hunter who met an accidental death near this spot. The marker was left by his family as a reminder to other hunters to be careful. The road follows Newby's Bay on Manitou Lake, which was named for the Newby family of Rockville. Alfred (1865–1941), his wife, Mary Ann Stevens (1869–1966), the first three of their nine children, Mary Ann's parents, and her grandmother settled here in 1895. Alfred Newby was a plasterer, and he and his sons had a lime kiln in the bush. In 1864 the area was the site of a very large sugarbush. Just northwest of where the road meets the lakeshore of Newby's Bay is the site of the Newby homestead. On the right, at the rural intersection, was a small log building. This unique masterpiece of log parquetry was built about 1908 by Major Newby as a playhouse for his young nieces Helen and Zella Newby. Constructed of small cedar poles, one side featured logs cut and placed in the form of the Union Jack flag. This unique structure was once home to the Newby family and later served as temporary shelter for families in need.

In this area in the mid-1860s two native families resided on the shore of Manitou Lake: the Peeyahbewaush family of eight and the Ahdick family of four. Anglican missionary Jabez Sims, a frequent visitor, wrote in his journal on 6 February 1865:

Fine day. I traveled with Andrew [Andrew Jacobs, his assistant] 30 miles to the other end of Manitou Lake and back to see Peeyahbewaush and Ahdick's families. Peter Ahwunahgwud took us: took them some four and corn. Arrived about 12 o'clock – Peeyahbewaush was fishing in the Lake (very bad going, snow slightly crusted over, water underneath). Found their wigwams very cleanly laid with fir boughs and mats for our reception. Held service in Ahdick's wigwam. Preached on the fall of man and his recovery to Christianity. I was requested to come again which I promised to do in 2 weeks and baptize 2 of Peeyahbewaush's children [William John and Mary Ann were subsequently baptized on 21 February 1865]. Ahdick proposes to stay, but Peeyahbewaush to go to Shegawaindoh in the spring. Returned home which we reached about 6 pm. On our way back Peter related the Oddawah tradition of the flood and part of the tradition of the Creation.

The Newby homestead featured a masterpiece of log parquetry.

A government dock and boat ramp provide access to Manitou Lake south of Rockville. The road meets the shore again at the Duck n' Drake Marine. Lehman's Landing, now known as Camp Mary Ann, was named for Abraham Lehman, who farmed here and operated a Lake Manitou ferry service for settlers. The post office here operated from 1880 to 1892 with Lehman as the postmaster. Take a sharp right at the Camp Mary Ann corner, marked by a huge frame barn. Then make a left turn 0.5 km farther on. The road encounters the lake again at the tiny hamlet of Gibraltar, where it heads south to meet Highway 542. The tour turns left at the highway, but you can turn right to go to Mindemoya for lunch. To continue the tour, turn left onto paved Highway 542 in the direction of the hamlet of Big Lake.

John and Dolly Cannard's cement house overlooked Big Lake.

The water on the right is Big Lake, which is separated from Manitou Lake by a half-kilometre of land. Opposite the lake was the former home of John and Dolly Cannard and their four children. Built in 1922 by John Cannard and a mason, the stately two-and-a-half storey cement home anchored the corner for over 70 years. A 'cement house' has a veneer of concrete over a standard wood frame. This treatment was relatively inexpensive, as lime for the cement was a local product.

Past the lake is the hamlet of Big Lake, which could claim to be settled by the Chambers sisters. In 1875 Mary Chambers (1854–1934) and her husband, Al Brown (1838–1917), settled here. They were followed a short time later by Agnes Chambers and her husband, J.H. Johnston (1846–1919), and Jeanette

Chambers with her husband, Charles Moody (born in 1850 in Yorkshire, England). The Moodys arrived on the steamer *Jane Miller*, the first steamboat built on Manitoulin. It was built in 1879 by the Miller brothers of Little Current and transported many pioneers to the island. The first sawmill was built around 1880 by blacksmith Robert Stapleton, who later built a mill at Budge's Settlement on Manitou Lake.

This is the Township of Sandfield, now part of the Township of Central Manitoulin. It was surveyed in 1870 and named for the Hon. John Sandfield Macdonald, joint premier of United Canada, 1862–4, and the first premier of Ontario, 1867–71. He was often called Sandfield, the family's Scottish subsurname, to distinguish him from the Hon. John A. Macdonald, Canada's first prime minister in 1867.

Silver Bay on Lake Manitou was, by 1880, a community of 35 families. That year the first school was built by Mr Keys for $120. The school burned in 1887 and was rebuilt by Henry and Robert Stapleton.

From Big Lake the road leads through maple bush, followed by flat grazing land scattered with rocks, stumps, cedars, and wildflowers. The settlement of Sandfield is located at the mouth of the Manitou River, on Manitou Lake's Sandfield Bay. It was the only one of the island's first eight settlements which was not located on a good harbour on the Lake Huron shore. Turn left on the Hutchinson side road to the shore of Manitou Lake and the river's mouth. Here you can see across the lake to the area where this tour began. A small island in the river's mouth (accessible by a bridge) is a pretty picnic spot. A boat ramp is also located here.

Stonemason Elias Hutchinson's stone house sits on the lakeshore. It was built in 1928 of lakeshore rocks. The Sandfield post office was established in 1880, with William McDonald, a flour and saw mill owner, as postmaster. McDonald was born in Perth, Ontario, in 1820 of Scottish parents. He and his wife, Loretta Harris, and their family settled in Manitowaning, where he was in partnership with John Purdy, moving here in the late 1870s to establish his mills. Initially, his sons helped run the mills; but in 1879 James Johnston from Pickering, Ontario, took over the sawmill. In 1880 Sandfield was a bustling community with grist, saw and shingle, carding, and woollen mills as well as a number of lime kilns in the vicinity. In one month alone, in the spring of 1880, four houses and five barns were raised. Watson's General Store has been operated since 1886 by five generations of Watsons. Samuel Watson and Lucinda Gough Watson, from Orangeville, Ontario, settled at Watson's Bay on Manitou Lake, near Sandfield, in 1872.

The Sandfield Fish Culture Station may be toured on weekdays. Manitoulin's first fish hatchery was created by the Manitou Fish Company, which leased Manitou Lake in 1903 as a whitefish fishing grounds. The establishment later became a bass and trout hatchery. The rearing ponds were built in 1937 and stocked for the first time the following year with 300,000 speckled trout yearlings. The facility now works in conjunction with the new Blue Jay Creek Fish Culture Station located to the south. Some of the Blue Jay's lake trout 'backcross' yearlings are transferred to Sandfield Station in the fall for winter rearing in the ponds. In the spring the 17-month-old fish, which are 15 cm (6 inches) long, are released in Manitoulin and North Shore waters.

Continuing southeast from Sandfield the road crosses briefly into Tehkummah Township. Tehkummah Township was established in 1866 and is named for Louis Tekoma, or Tehkummah (described in the Eastern Bays chapter). Just west of here on tiny Snow Lake is the hamlet of Snowville, which was named for the Snow family. William B. Snow and his bride, Miss Bennett, walked ten miles to their new home, a log shanty with a mud floor, after their wedding at Hilly Grove. At the junction of Highway 542A a short detour will take you into the hamlet of Tehkummah.

Tehkummah post office was established in 1874 with Samuel R. McKewan as the first postmaster. Sam, a 38-year-old Ontario-born farmer of Scottish descent, settled here in 1873 with his family. Fairview United Church was built in 1897 with donations of lumber, shingles, and labour. A large stable, practically a necessity for all churches until the age of the automobile, was originally located next to the building. The adjacent cemetery was donated to the Methodists in 1880 by John Dawson, who was born in Ireland around 1822 and who lived here with his large family. This area is composed of beautiful rolling farmland. In the hamlet are Ward's General Store, established in 1907 by J. Ward, and the Wood'n It Be Nice gift shop.

Return to the Highway 542 intersection and turn right. On the immediate left is the Blue Jay Creek hatchery, which opened in 1990. Lake trout and a splake/trout cross called 'backcross' are raised here. It is one of fifteen provincial fish hatcheries in Ontario. Fresh water is continuously supplied by the adjacent Blue Jay Creek springs. The hatchery is designed specifically for egg incubation and early rearing. Every year in the fall the hatchery collects about 3.5 million eggs of lake trout and lake trout backcross from fish caught by nets in Manitou Lake. The eggs are disinfected, incubated for about sixty days, hatched, and then, thirty days after hatching, transferred to troughs. When the troughs are outgrown, about two-thirds of the fingerlings are moved to the raceways. In May one-half million backcross move on to the provincial Cage Culture Site, just north of Little Current. The rest remain here until fall, when they go to the Sandfield facility. The following spring, 17 months after the eggs were collected, the fish are released to stock the waters of Manitoulin and the North Shore.

Next to the hatchery, across the creek, a stone cairn marks the site of the area's first sawmill. On the creek bed are the timber remains of the mill dam. This sawmill was built in 1880 for Frank Bowler by Manitowaning contractor John Purdy. Bowler, a farmer born in Ontario around 1849, settled here with his wife, Margaret, and their three children. In 1908 the mill was sold to John McGauley. Around 1890 Tehkummah's first lime kiln was operated by Jim Cooper on the property of James Dawson. A small kiln, it produced only about one hundred bushels per firing.

From the hatchery, continue southeast on Highway 542 until it intersects Highway 6, where you turn left to Manitowaning and Little Current or right to South Baymouth.

References

Unpublished sources

Archives of Ontario. Strachan papers
Canada. Census of Canada, 1851–1891
Environment Canada, Parks Service. Canadian Inventory of Historic
  Building
Federal Heritage Buildings Review Office. Building Reports
Guinon, Charles E. (editor, *Manitoulin Expositor*, 1960s). Research
  papers. Private colln
Historic Sites and Monuments Board of Canada. Agenda papers
Hornick, ed. 'How it all began: a history of the Kagawong area, circa
  1872–1910.' Vol. 1 of 2 vols., n.d. Kagawong, Ont., Public Library.
  Photocopy
Missions to the Ojibwe Indians: Letters from Rev. Frederick O'Meara
  and others. Wilberforce Eames Indian Collection. Manuscript Divi-
  sion, New York Public Library
Myers, Frank A. Research papers. Private colln
National Archives of Canada. Department of Indian Affairs. Record
  Group 10
National Archives of Canada. Missionary and Church Records. Manu-
  script Group 3
O'Flaherty, Father J. Edward, SJ. Research papers, place-names. Private
  colln

Sims, Rev. Jabez Waters. Journal and correspondence, 1863–8.
National Archives of Canada. Pre-Confederation records. Manuscript Group 24, J51

Sims, Rev. Jabez Waters, Thomas Chapman Sims, Charles Latin Dupont
Sims, Francis Lyle Sims, Wilfrid Alan (Bill) Sims. Papers, 1864 to
1985. Private colln

Published sources

Aboriginal Protection Society. *Report on the Indians of Upper Canada.*
London, 1839

Barry, J.C. *Georgian Bay, the Sixth Great Lake.* Toronto: Clarke Irwin,
1968

Blumenson, John. *Ontario Architecture: A Guide to Styles and Building
Terms, 1784 to the Present.* Markham, Ont.: Fitzhenry and Whiteside,
1990

Burt, Elda. *Portraits of Manitoulin's Past.* Gore Bay, Ont.: Mid-North
Printers and Publishers, n.d.

Canada, Indian treaties and surrenders from 1680–1890. Ottawa, 1891

Canada, Journals of the Legislative Assembly of the Province of Canada

*Canada, Sessional papers and annual reports of the departments of Indian
Affairs, Public Works, Marine and Fisheries*

The Canadian Indian. Ottawa: Ministry of Indian Affairs and Northern
Development, 1986

The Canadian Indian: Ontario. Ottawa: Ministry of Indian Affairs and
Northern Development, 1982

Carter, F.E. *Place Names of Ontario.* 2 vols. London, Ont.: Phelps,
1984

Chapman, L.J., and D.F. Putnam. *The Physiography of Southern Ontario.*
2d ed. Toronto: University of Toronto Press, 1966

Coyne, J.H. 'Across Georgian Bay in 1871.' *Ontario Historical Society
Papers and Records* 28 (1932): 25–9

Cumberland, Barlow, ed. *The Northern Lakes of Canada.* Toronto: Hunter,
Rose & Co., 1886

Disturnell, John. *A Trip Through the Lakes of North America.* New York:
J. Disturnell, 1857

Fox, Mary Lou. *The Way It Was, an Ojibwe-Odawa Legend.* West Bay,
Ont.: Ojibwe Cultural Foundation, 1979

Harker, Douglas E. *The Woodwards.* Vancouver: Mitchell Press, 1976

A History and Guide of the Church of Saint Francis of Assisi. Mindemoya, Ont., n.d.

Immaculate Conception Church. Pamphlet. West Bay, Ont., n.d.

Jameson, Mrs. *Winter Studies and Summer Rambles in Canada*. 2 vols. New York: Wiley and Putnam, 1977

Jenness, Diamond. *The Indians of Canada*. 7th ed. Toronto: University of Toronto Press, 1977

Johnston, Basil. *Ojibway Heritage*. Toronto: McClelland and Stewart, 1976

Kane, Paul. *Sketch Pad*. Toronto: Musson, 1969

– *Wanderings of an artist among the Indians of North America, from Canada to Vancouver's Island and Oregon through the Hudson's Bay Companies territory and back again*. Edmonton: M.G. Hurtig, 1968

Kingston, William H.G. *Western Wanderings or, a Pleasure Tour in the Canadas*. London: Chapman and Hall; Montreal: B. Dawson, 1856

Landon, Fred. *Lake Huron*. Indianapolis: Bobbs-Merrill, 1944

McQuarrie, W. John. *The Early Years of Gore Bay*. Gore Bay, Ont.: The Manitoulin Recorder, 1990

MacRae, Marion, and Anthony Adamson. *The Ancestral Roof: Domestic Architecture of Upper Canada*. Toronto: Clarke Irwin, 1963

Major, Frederick Wm. *Manitoulin, the Isle of the Ottawas*. Gore Bay, Ont.: Recorder Press, 1934

The *Manitoulin Expositor*. Little Current, Ont.: Manitoulin Publishing Co. Ltd., 1879–present

The *Manitoulin Recorder*. Gore Bay, Ont. (And predecessors extant)

Mer Douce, the Georgian Bay Magazine (The Algonquin Historical Society) 1 (May 1921) to 12 (Sept. 1923)

Mika, Nick, and Helma Mika. *Place Names of Ontario*. 3 vols. Belleville: Mika, 1977

Mihinnick, Jeanne. *At Home in Upper Canada*. Toronto: Clarke, Irwin, 1983

Morton, J.K. *The Flora of Manitoulin Island and Adjacent Islands of Lake Huron, Georgian Bay and the North Channel*. Waterloo: University of Waterloo, Department of Biology, 1977

Oliphant, Laurence. *Minnesota and the far West*. Edinburgh, London: W. Blackwood, 1855

Ontario. Annual reports of the departments of Public Works, Agriculture. Toronto

Patterson, E.P. *The Canadian Indian*. Don Mills, Ont.: Collier-Macmillan Canada, 1972

Putnam, D.F. 'Manitoulin Island.' *Geographic Review* 37 (1947): 649–62

Remarks on Upper Canada Surveys and Extracts from the Surveyor's Report ... in the Ottawa River and Georgian Bay Section. Ottawa: Hunter, Rose and Co., 1867

Rempel, John I. *Building with Wood*, rev. ed. Toronto: University of Toronto Press, 1980

Ritchie, Thomas. *Canada Builds.* Toronto: University of Toronto Press, 1967

Rosenthal, Max. 'Manitoulin Island: 65 Years of Postal History.' *British North American Philatelic Society Journal*, May 1971 and June 1971

Saunders, William E. *Diaries of a Trip to Manitoulin Island (1880) and of a Trip down the Thames River (1881).* London, Ont.: London Public Library and Art Museum, 1974

Sprock, A.F. 'The Norisle of Owen Sound and Tobermory.' *Inland Sea* 22 (1966): 318–20

Theberge, John B., ed. *Legacy, the Natural History of Ontario.* Toronto: McClelland and Stewart, 1989

Through the Years: Manitoulin District History and Genealogy. Gore Bay, Ont.: Mid-North Printers and Publishers, Nov. 1983–present

White, J. 'Place-names of Georgian Bay including the North Channel.' *Ontario History* 12 (1911): 5–81

Wightman, W.R. *Forever on the Fringe: Six Studies in the Development of Manitoulin Island.* Toronto: University of Toronto Press, 1982

Index

Italic numbers refer to illustrations.

Abbotossway, Charles 64
Abbotossway, George 45, 46, 64
Abitibi Power and Paper
  Company 37
Adawish, Vincent 150
Advance 85
Agricultural Museum 189
Ahdick family 206
Ahwunagwud, Peter 11, 31, 206
Ainslie, James D. and Bridget
  106
airport, Eastern Manitoulin 170
airport, Gore Bay 99
Algoma Eastern Railway 20, 48
Algoma Eastern Terminals Ltd.
  48, 49
Algoma sidewheeler 13
Algonquin 3, 4, 5, 128
Allan, Hon. George William 83
Allan Township 83
Anderson, Charles 47, 52, 54
Anderson, John 163

Anglican Church of Saint Francis
  of Assisi 190, *190*
archaeological sites: Michael's
  Bay 131; Providence Bay 128;
  Sheguiandah 176
architecture 33–6; house construction techniques 33–6;
  house styles 34; log houses
  33, 153, *154*, *207*; pioneer
  cabins 180–2; tipis 155; trough
  roof 83, 181; wigwamace 104,
  175
arrival of Europeans 4
Asia steamship 15, 74
Assiginack, Francis and Benjamin 145
Assiginack, John-Baptiste 110,
  145
Assiginack Township 145
Atkinson, John and Francis 63,
  179, 202
Aundeck Omni Akaning (Where

the crows live) or Sucker Creek
First Nation 29, 46, 63–5
Aylesworth, Charles 177, 178

Bailey family 105
Baker, John B. 124
Ball, Hector and Jim 114
Barrie Island 99–101, *101*
Batman, Thomas James and
Evangeline Agnew 176–7,
202
Bay of Islands 39
Behulah Methodist Church 126
Belanger Bay 109
Bell Rock 40–1, *41*
Bellwood, W.A.M. 49, 53
Berry, Oliver 81
Berry boats 81, 82
Bezwah or Buzwah, Jean-
Baptiste, Sr 149
bicycling xii, 68, 170
Bidwell 201
Bidwell, Hon. Marshall Spring
66, 202
Bidwell Township 66, 201–2
Big Lake 208
Billings, Elkanah 68
Billings Church 73
Billings Schools No. 1 and No. 2
73
Billings Township 68
Birch Island 39
bird-watching xv, 99
Blue Jay Creek Fish Culture Sta-
tion 210, 211
Bond Head, Lieutenant-Gover-
nor Francis 6
Bowler, Frank 211
Bowman, Beniah 85

Bowser, Thomas and Sarah
Hutchinson 73
Boyd, William, Annie, and Vera
78
Boyter, Robert and Isabella 98
Brailey, Bob, viewpoint 180
Bridal Veil Falls 74, *75*
Bridal Veil Falls hiking trail 74
Britainville 126
Britainville Church 126
Britten, George and Clara 22, 143
Budge, John 197
Budge's Settlement 197
Burkitt, John 45
Burnett Hill 180
'Burning Boat' 129
Burnt Island 108–9
Burpee, Isaac 105
Burpee Township 105
Buzwah 29, 149

cabbage heads 135
Campbell, Sir Alexander 125
Campbell, Colin and Isaac 104
Campbell Bay 102, *103*, 104
Campbell Township 125
Cannard, John and Dolly 208
Cape Robert lighthouse 110
Caribou ferry 19, *19*, 22, 23, 142,
165
Carnarvon–Billings Line trail
195
Carnarvon Municipal Park 188
Carnarvon–Tehkummah Line
trail 130–1
Carter, James 76, 80–2
Carter Bay 130, *132*
Catholic cemetery, North Chan-
nel Drive 53

cedar shingles 73, 168
cement houses 36, 170, 208, *208*
Centre Hall or Centre Gable
    house 34, *100*
Chambers sisters (Mary, Agnes,
    Jeanette) 208–9
Champlain, Samuel de 4
Chatreau, Luke 76, 87
Chi-Cheemaun ferry 24, 143, *143*,
    165
Chicora steamship 13, 14
Clarke, Stewart 93, 99, 102, 113
Cockburn Island 117
Cold Springs cemetery and St
    Andrew's Presbyterian
    Church 67, *68*
Columbus, James, or Ooshke-
    wahbik 45, 46, 64–5
Columbus Mountain 64
Colville's Woolly Harvest farm
    121–4
Conlon, J. & T. 54
Cook, John and Ellen 107
Cooke, Elizabeth 189
Cook's Bay 107
Cooper, Jim 211
Corbiere, Lance Corporal Austin
    Morris 60
Corbiere, George, Henry, and
    Mary 71
corduroy roads 68
Coyne, J.H. 14
Creation, the 31–2
Cup and Saucer Hiking Trail
    66–7, *67*

Davis, Dr Robert 191
Dawson, John (builder) 52
Dawson, John (farmer) 210–11

Dawson, Simon J. 110
Dawson Township 110
De-ba-jeh-mu-jig (storyteller)
    Theatre 156
deer 83, 135–6, 180
Demi, Adam and Jane 205
desertion of the island (1651–2) 5
Disturnell, John 13
Dodge, Daniel (Danny) George
    81–2
dolomite rock 84–5, 115
Dreamer's Rock 29, 39, *40*
drumlins 84
Dryden's Corner 127
Duck Islands 107, 109, 124
Duncanson, John and Cather-
    ine 107
Dunlop, John and Mary May 66,
    202
Dupont, Charles Latin 7, 8

E.B. Eddy Forest Products Ltd
    38
Eastern Bays 139
Edmonds, John and Margaret
    108
Edowishkosh 110
Elizabeth Bay *105*, 105–6
Espanola 37–8
'Establishment' at Manito-
    waning 7, 150, 158
Evans, Frank 126
Evans, John 195
Evansville 104
events: Central Manitoulin Lions
    Club Fiddler's Jamboree 188;
    Haweater Weekend 55; La
    Cloche Country Art Show 38;
    Manitowaning Summerfest

and fall fair 165; Mindemoya
Homecoming Weekend 188;
Perch Derby 128; Providence
Bay Annual Fair 127; Shegui-
andah Powwow 173; Sucker
Creek Day 64; West Bay Pow-
wow 71, *72*; Wikwemikong
Powwow 155

Fairview United Church 210
Falls, Thomas 113
farming 84
Farquhar, Thomas and Jane
Nixon 189
Farthing, Henry and Robert
108
Ferguson, John and Mary Ann
203
Ferguson, Lindsay and Sarah
Stringer 202
ferry between South Baymouth
and Tobermory 21–2, 23, 24,
142–3, *143*
Fisher, James 126
fishing xv, 82, 107, 108–9, 112,
140
Fossil Hill 146
Four Square house 34, *208*
Foxey 101–2
Frances Smith steamship 14, 17
Fraser, Henry Charles 180
Fraser, James M. 88
Frost, Rev. Canon Frederick 32,
145

Gallagher, George 124
Gamey, Robert 85, 92
gardening on Manitoulin 149
Garland, Thomas 128

Gibraltar 207
Gimoshkam, Michael 150
Goat Island 42, 48, *49*
golf courses: Espanola 38; Gore
Bay 99; Mindemoya 188;
Manitowaning/ Wikwe-
mikong 149; Tehkummah
(miniature) 144–5
Gordon, Hon. James 99
Gordon Township 99
Gordon's Park 144–5
Gore Bay 85–94, *87, 88, 91, 94*;
All Saints Anglican Church
95; Community Hall 93; court-
house 90, *91*; East Bluff Look-
out *94*, 98; golf course 99;
incorporated as a town 89;
Lyons Memorial Church 95;
Manitoulin Recorder 94; Munic-
ipal Building and Library 89;
museum 99; picnic area and
playground 89; post office 93;
tourist information at marina
pavilion 85
Gore steamship 12
Gow, Peter 15–16
Gray, George R. 37
Great Duck Island 109
Great Northern Transit Company
16, 18
Green Bay 202–3
Green Bay United Church 203
Griffon, wreck of the 90, 116–17
Grimes, Samuel 126
Grimsthorpe 126

Hagey, Daniel 195
Halcrow, James and Theresa
Helen Hale Nicholson 170–1

Hall, Willard and Jane Dinsmore 87
Harbour Centre building, Providence Bay 130
Hartley, George 127
Hastie, John and Margaret Roszel 178
Haweater 55
Henry, Alexander, Sr 40
Henry, George 76
Henry, Robert and William 74–6
High Falls picnic area 168, *169*
hiking trails: Bridal Veil Falls Hiking Trail 74; Carnarvon–Billings Line trail 195; Carnarvon–Tehkummah Line trail 130–1; Cup and Saucer Hiking Trail 66–7; Gordon's Park 144; Lewis Twin Peaks 175; M'Chigeeng Hiking Trails 71; McLean Park 145; Orr Mountain 179; Rainbow Trail 38
Hilliard, John 18, 79
Hilly Grove 148
Hilly Grove Pioneer Chapel 148
Hindman, Howard 135
Holy Cross Mission Church 153
Holy Trinity Anglican Cemetery 60
honey 65
Honora Bay 65
Hope Farm 191
Hope Lumber Company 54
Hopetown 191
Howell, Alexander 191
Howland, Hon. Sir William Pierce 60
Howland Township 60
Hudson's Bay Company 40, 45

Huron 4, 5
Hutchinson, Elias 209

Ice Lake 83
Immaculate Conception Church, M'Chigeeng 69–70, *70*
Indian Point Bridge 102, 121
Ireton, Samuel 124
Iroquois 3–5

Jacobs, Rev. Peter 158
Jameson, Anna Brownell 11, 150
Jane Miller, the first steamboat built on Manitoulin 209
Janet Head lighthouse *93*, 98
Jenkins, Stuart 49, 51
Jesuits at Wikwemikong. *See* missionaries
Johnston, J.H. 209
Johnston, James 209
Jones, Hon. Robert 52

Kaboni 156
Kagawong 74–82; Anglican Church of St John the Evangelist *79*, 80; Havelock Hotel 18, 78–9; Hunt's Store 80; Manitoulin Pulp Company mill 80; St Paul on the Hill 82
Kagawong cemetery 80
Kagawong lighttower 81
Kalamazoo Vegetable Parchment Company 38
Kaloolah sidewheeler 12
Kane, Paul 12
Kasheese Studio 69
Keeshkakkoo, Thomas 139–40
Kezis, Chief Edahwe 173, 175
Kingsbury, George 50

Kingston, William H.G. 12
Kinochemeg 150
Kitche Manitou xiv, 31–2, 39, 187

La Cloche Mountains xiv, 37–8
La Cloche Peninsula 39
La Salle, René-Robert Cavalier
    Sieur de 116–17
Lake Kagawong 74, 82
Lake Nipissing, ancient shoreline
    of 121
Lake Wolsey 102, 124
Latta, Archibald 100
Layton, Dr S. 166
legends, native xiv, 31–2, 187–8
Legg, William 127
Lehman, Abraham 207
Lehman, Jesse 78
lighthouses 81, 98, 109, 115–16,
    142, 166, 179
Lily Lake settlement 201
lime kilns 35–6, 203–4, 204, 206,
    211
Little Current 14, 43–55, 46, 50;
    Anchor Inn 50; Holy Trinity
    Anglican Church 52; Hud-
    son's Bay Company post 45;
    incorporated as a town 51; Lit-
    tle Current Planing Mill (Red
    Mill) 47, 54, 54; lockup, former
    53; *Manitoulin Expositor* 49;
    Manitoulin Health Centre 55;
    Manitoulin Tourist Informa-
    tion Centre xv, 48; Mansion
    House 18, 50, 50; Merchant's
    Bank of Canada 50–1; mills
    47, 54–5; Picnic Island Mill
    54–5; post office 51; St Ber-
    nard's Catholic Church 53;

St Vincent de Paul Catholic
    Church 53; 'Sawdust Town'
    47; Spider Island Marina 54;
    swing bridge 47, 47–8; Turner
    Park 55; Turner's store 49–50;
    United Church 52; War Me-
    morial 51; Water Street 49
Little Current–Howland Muse-
    um (now the Centennial Muse-
    um of Sheguiandah) 175
Little Rapids Pulp Company 80
Little Red Schoolhouse museum
    142
Lonely Bay 126
Lyon, Robert A. 133, 134, 148
Lyon, William D. 133

M'Chigeeng (West Bay) 69–73;
    Immaculate Conception
    Church 69–70, 70; Kasheese
    Studio 69; native art 69;
    native settlement in 1847 69;
    Ojibwe Cultural Founda-
    tion 71; powwow 29, 72,
    72–3
M'Chigeeng (formerly West Bay
    First Nation) 69
M'Chigeeng Hiking Trails *ii*, 71
McCormick, William 126
Macdonald, John Sandfield 209
MacDonald, Laurine 81
McDonald, William and Loretta
    Harris 209
McDougall, William 7
McKenzie, Donald and Margaret
    Maria 60
McKeown, William 88
McKewan, Samuel R. 210
Mackie, Brian or Bryan 13, 53

McLean, Donald and Sarah Mc-
Kechnie 145
McLean, Donald E. 145
McLean, Hector 89
McLean, John 62
McLean, Samuel and Mary 61, 62
McLean Park 145–6, *147*
McLean's Mountain lookout 61,
62
McNiven, John R. 128
McQuarrie, John Hector 88
Maiangowi, Louis 156
Manitou and Northshore Rail-
way 47
Manitou River 131, 133, 135
Manitoulin Expositor 14–15, 49,
159, 161
Manitoulin Health Centre 55
Manitoulin Ranch and Lumber
Company 112
Manitoulin Recorder, founding
of 94
Manitoulin Ski Club 65
Manitoulin steamship and ferry
15, 20, 22, 24, 74
Manitoulin Tourist Information
Centre xv, 29, 43, 48
Manitoulin Transport Inc. 99
Manitowaning 158–68; annual
presentation to natives 11–12,
166–8; Assiginack Museum
161–2, *162*; Burns Wharf
Theatre *164*, 165; the 'Estab-
lishment' 7, 158; Manitoulin
Roller Mills 163–5, *164*; Mas-
tin's store 161–2; *Norisle*
ferry *164*, 165; St Paul's
Church 166, *167*; United
Church 161

Manitowaning Bay 156–8
Manitowaning lighthouse 166
Manitowaning Planing Mills 163
Manitowaning Treaty (1862) 7,
159
Maple Point or Maimonakeking
81
Martin, William McFall (memo-
rial to) 206
Mastin, Arthur and Catherine
Reynolds 162
May, Humphrey 52, 111–12
May, John T. 49
May, Philip and Amelia 61
Meldrum Bay 111–13; 'Fish Box
Bay' 112; Manitoulin Ranch
and Lumber Company mill
112; Meldrum Bay Inn 111,
113; Net Shed Museum 112;
Outfitter Store 113
Mennonite Brethren in Christ
Church 127
Meyers, John and Elizabeth
Ponting 171
Michael's Bay 131–5
Mills, Hon. David 121
Mills/Burpee Cemetery 124
Mills Township 105, 121
Mills United Church 125
Mindemoya 188–91; Agricul-
tural Museum 189–90; Angli-
can Church of Saint Francis of
Assisi *190*, 190–1; annual
homecoming weekend 188;
Brookwood Brae golf course
188; dairy industry 189; Hope
Farm 191; Red Cross Hospital,
former 191
Mindemoya Lake 185, *187*

Mindemoya Lake Cave 127, 193–5, *194*
mink and silver fox ranching 109
Misery Bay 106
missionaries: Jesuits at Wikwemikong 4, 5, 6, 7, 150, 153; Roman Catholic 4–5, 150
Mississagi Strait lighthouse *114, 115,* 115–16, *116*
Mit-ig-o-mish (medicine man) 39
Mizhequongi, High Chief John 159, 173
Mizhequongi, Margaret 175
Mocosik, Joseph 149
Montizambert, Rev. Canon Eric 64
Monument Corner *192,* 193
Moody, Charles 209
Moquam, Old John, or Otchonomequom 88, 104
Moquam, Johnny, or Endahsoogwameb 104
Morrison, John 189
Morrisville 109
museums: Agricultural Museum, Mindemoya 189–90; Assiginack Museum, Manitowaning 161, *162*; Centennial Museum of Sheguiandah (formerly Little Current–Howland Museum) 175, 176; Gore Bay museum 90; Harbour Centre building, Providence Bay 130; Kagawong postal 78; Little Red Schoolhouse museum, South Baymouth 142; Mindemoya Pioneer Park 189; Mississagi Strait lighthouse *114, 115,* 115–16, *116*; Net Shed Mu-seum, Meldrum Bay 112
Mutchmor, Ralph W. and John W. 128
Myers, Frank A. 104, 195

Nanabush 32, 187–8. *See also* legends, native
narrowest point on the island 124
native rights and territory 6
Nelson, John and Lizzie Wilson 83
Newby, Alfred and Mary Ann Stevens 205, 206, *207*
Newby's Bay 206
Newman, Sarah 45
Niagara Escarpment xiv, 63, 66–7, *67,* 144
Nindawayma ferry 24, 143
Nineteen Lake 108
Noland, Edward 124, 125
Norgoma ferry 24, 142
Norisle ferry 23, 24, 142–3, *164,* 165
Normac ferry 22, 24, 113, 117, 142, 165
north coast of Manitoulin 57
North Shore Navigation Company 18
North West Company 40

Odawa 4, 6, 102, 128, 131
Odjig, Dominic 153, 156
Odjig-Fisher, Rosemary (Peltier) 26
O'Flaherty, Father J. Edward, SJ 109, 170
oil 151, 178–9, 202

Ojibwe 3–4, 102
Ojibwe Cultural Foundation, M'Chigeeng 71
Old Spring Bay 126, 193
Oliphant, Laurence 12
Ombidjiwang 102–4
O'Meara, Rev. Frederick A. 166, 173
Ontario Fisheries Research Station 144
Ontario Northland Transportation Commission 142
Ontario Paper Company 110
Owen family 126
Owen Sound Transportation Company 20, 21–2, 142

Paimsahdung 144
Parkinson, Joshua and Mary Jane 205
Parkinson, Wells 205
Patten, T.J. 43, 53
Peeyahbewaush family 206
Perivale 126
Perivale Gallery 126
Phillips, Alfred, Abraham, and Peter 126
Poncet, Father Joseph 5, 170
Poplar 125
Poplar War Memorial 125
Poquam, Jim, or Bai-gum-quoum 102
Portage Lake 124
Potts, Miss 49, 53
powwow 25–9, 28, 64, 72, 110, 155–6, 157, 173
Proulx, Father Jean-Baptiste 150
Providence Bay 127–30; archaeological site 128; beach 130,
131; Harbour Centre building 130; legends 129; St Peter's Anglican chapel 130; timbering 128–9
Providence Bay Milling Company 128
Purdy, John 163, 209, 211
Purvis, George 109
Purvis, William and Ann Frost 109
Purvis Brothers Fishery 108–9

Queen Elizabeth the Queen Mother M'Nidoo M'Nissing Provincial Park (QUNO) 109

Rainbow Gardens 148–9
Rainbow Trail 38
Reynolds, Catherine 162
Reynolds, John 162
Rivett, Robert and Ann 80
roads, development of 8, 20–1, 148, 180, 200
Robinson, Hon. John Beverly 106
Robinson Township 106
Rock Garden Terrace Resort 127, 193, 195
Rockville 205
Rockville Grace United Church 205
Roosevelt Memorial 39
Route of the Voyageurs 40
Rowe, William 61
Rowe settlement 65
Runnalls, Lewis 101
Runnalls, Percy and Effie Hern 100

Runnalls, William Nelson and
    Catherine Ann Rowe 84, 100
Runnalls, William O. *100*, 100
Rutledge, John 148

'Sailor's Grave' 129
St Andrew's United Church,
    Robinson Township 107–8
St Gabriel Lalement Church 39
St Luke's Anglican Church,
    Sucker Creek 64
St Peter's Anglican Church, Sil-
    ver Lake 108
Salem Missionary Church 126–7
Samigokwe, Mary Ann 145
sand dunes 109, 124, 130, *132*
Sandfield 209
Sandfield Fish Culture Station
    210
Sandfield Township 209
Saunders, Edwin (Ned) 87, 106
Saunders, William 88, 106
Saunders, William Edwin 15, 91
Schroeder, William 127, 195
Scott, John 125
Seabrook, Jack, Agricultural
    Museum 189
Sears-Roebuck catalogues 80
settlement of Manitoulin 3–9;
    land first offered for sale (1866)
    8, 9, 13; pre-European 3–5
Sheguiandah 170–9; ancient
    quartz quarry 176; Batman's
    mill replica 176, *177*; Centen-
    nial Museum of Sheguiandah
    (former Little Current–How-
    land Museum) 175; mills 176–
    7; picnic area, boat launch, and
    government dock 178; pow-

wow 29, 173; residents in
    1865 175; settlement 148; St
    Andrew's Anglican Church
    173–4, *174*; United Church 178
Sheguiandah Bay 172–3
Sheguiandah First Nation 171,
    173–5
Sheguiandah Township 170, 200
Sheppard, Albert and Elisa 205
Sheppard, W.J. 37
Shesheguaning First Nation 29,
    109–10
Side Hall house 34, *35*
Sides, Thomas 125
silos 84, *95*, 99
Silver Bay 209
Silver Water 107–8
Sim, Robert 148
Simon, James Mishibinijima 149
Sims, Bill *21*, 193
Sims, Rev. Jabez Waters 8, 45, 52,
    139, 149, 173, 174, 175, 180–2
Sims, Thomas Chapman 51, 55
Skippen, John and Elizabeth Ann
    203
Skippen's Settlement 203
Slash settlement 146
Smith, W.L. 49, 161
Smyth, George and Henry 108
snake fences 63, *133*
Society of Jesus (Jesuits) at Wik-
    wemikong. *See* missionaries
South Bay West, or Chitewaie-
    gunning 146, 148
South Baymouth 139–44; ferry
    142, *143*; John Budd Memorial
    Park 144; Little Red School-
    house museum 142; Ontario
    Fisheries Research Station 144;

St Andrew's-by-the-Sea
United Church 142; St John's
Anglican Church 142; Teh-
kummah Township public
beach 144
Southern Route 121
Spanish River Paper Company
37
Spring Bay 126, 193
Sproat, William and Mary 146–8
Spry, Mrs Alfred (Lily) 205
Spry, James H. and Sarah 205
Stapleton, Robert 200, 209
Steiner, Bernard C. 18–19
Stoddard, Maitland, and Rixon
Co. 200
storm beach ridges 135
Strain, George 50, 92–3
Strawberry Island, or Appissa-
bikokaning 180
Stringer, Elizabeth 202
Stringer, James 62–3, 202
Sucker Creek First Nation or
Aundeck Omni Akaning
(Where the crows live) 29, 46,
63–5
Sucker Lake First Nation 168
swing bridge, Little Current 20,
23, 47, 47, 47–48

Taylor, Rev. Richard Martin 190–
1
Tecumseh Trail 107, 108
Tehkummah 210
Tehkummah, Louis 144, 210
Tehkummah Township 144,
210
Ten Mile Point 5, 170, 171
Thorburn, James M. 88

Thorburn, Robert 88
Thorburn, William 113
Tinkis, Douglas A. or 'Dunc' 50
Tinkis, Jehiel 18, 50
tipis 155
Tolsma, S.F. (Zebe) 117
Toronto Lumber Company 134
Tourist Information xv, 43, 48
Treaty, 1836 6, 158
Treaty, Manitowaning (1862) 7,
159
trough roof 83, 181
Tully, Kivas 91–2, 161
Turner, Barney, Byron H., and
Grant 52
Turner, Isaac and Elizabeth
Hawkins 49, 52
Twin Cedars cemetery 203
Two O'Clock 149

Vanzant's Landing 197
Vermeesch, Archie 53
Vidal Bay 110

Wabenasemin, Chief 139
Wacausia native camp 107
Wagg, Colman 188, 191
Wagg, Francis (Frank) 188, 189
Wagg, Tom 189
Wahbegagkake, James 158
Wakegiijik or Wakegijig, Chief
Louis 150, 155
Walker, Joseph 176
Walkhouse side-road 107
Wallace, Rev. W.E. 53
war memorials 51, 125, 153, 155,
193
Watson, Samuel and Lucinda
Gough 210

Waubano steamship 13, 15

West Bay. *See* M'Chigeeng

Western Manitoulin Historical
  Society 90

Wewebjiwang 43, 45

White, George 193

White, George and Maribah
  Sickles 180

Whitefish Falls 38–9

Whitefish River First Nation or
  Wawaskingaga 29, 38–9

White's Point 180

Wickett, George 113

wigwamace 104, 175

Wikwemikong 149–58; Amik-
  ook Gahmic, or Elder's Centre
  153; Health Centre *151*, 153;
  Holy Cross Mission Church
  153; Jennesseaux Hall 154;

Jesuit day school and residence 154; Odjig residence
  156; population in 1842 and
  1846 150; powwow 29, 155–6,
  157; Rainbow Lodge Recovery
  Centre 153

Wikwemikong Peninsula, settlement of 6, 150

Wikwemikong wilderness camps
  156

Wikwemikongsing 156

Willisville 38

Wilman, Val and Lovina 140

Wolsey Lake 102

Woodward, Charles 163, 201

Zhiibaahaasing (formerly Cockburn Island First Nation) 29,
  109, 110, 117